Meeting Places:
Locating Desert Consciousness in Performance

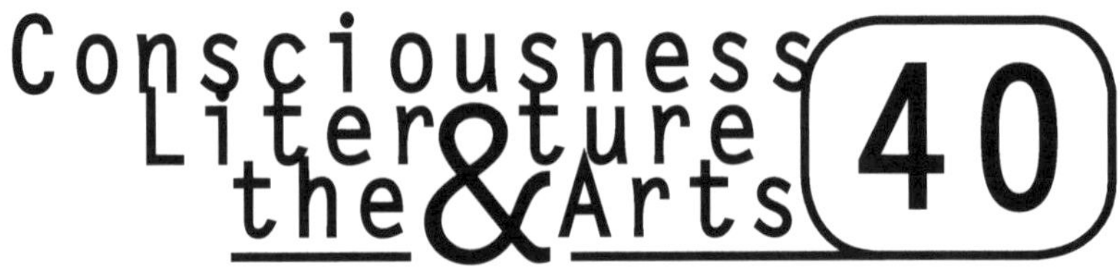

General Editor:
Daniel Meyer-Dinkgräfe

Editorial Board:
Anna Bonshek, Per Brask, John Danvers,
William S. Haney II, Amy Ione,
Michael Mangan, Arthur Versluis,
Christopher Webster, Ralph Yarrow
Jade Rosina McCutcheon

Meeting Places:
Locating Desert Consciousness in Performance

Mary Elizabeth Anderson

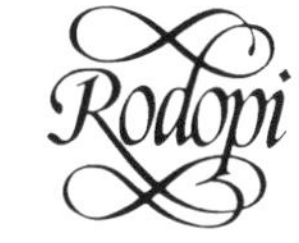

Amsterdam - New York, NY 2014

Cover illustration: *Spinifex*, © Richard Haley.

Cover design by Aart Jan Bergshoeff.

The paper on which this book is printed meets the requirements of "ISO 9706:1994, Information and documentation - Paper for documents - Requirements for permanence".

ISBN: 978-90-420-3849-3
ISSN: 1573-2193
E-Book ISBN: 978-94-012-1092-8
E-book ISSN: 1879-6044
© Editions Rodopi B.V., Amsterdam - New York, NY 2014
Printed in the Netherlands

Contents

Acknowledgments

My deep gratitude and thanks go to the many individuals and organizations that have made this project possible. The journey began with Ian Maxwell at the University of Sydney, who introduced me to the work of Tess de Quincey and put me into contact with her. Russell Emerson, Paul Dwyer, Gay McAuley, Amanda Card and Lowell Lewis also shared their knowledge and skills generously. De Quincey Company members and associated artists kindly shared their work, their thoughts and their experiences: *thank you* Tess de Quincey, Linda Luke, Peter Fraser, Victoria Hunt, Tina Harrison, Tom Davies, Vic McEwan, Sam James, Francesca da Rimini, Stuart Grant, Karen Vedel, Jim Denley, Richard Manner, Mayu Kanamori and Diana Knudsen.

I first developed writing in response to my experience as an intern with the De Quincey Company at UC Davis, under the guidance of Barbara Sellers-Young, Jade McCutcheon and Jon Rossini, who cultivated my thinking on the project in integral ways. A UC Davis Humanities award, followed by a University of California Office of the President Dissertation Fellowship, and finally a Fulbright Scholarship from the Australian-American Fulbright Commission enabled me to take a series of short- and long-term research trips to Australia. Portions of the prologue first appeared in *About Performance*, portions of chapter three appeared in *Brolga*, and portions of the epilogue appeared in *Canadian Journal of Practice-based Research in Theatre*. I am grateful to the editors and reviewers of those publications for helping to extend my thinking in those spaces. At Wayne State University, I have been supported by great colleagues as well as funding from the Humanities Center. Thanks especially to Doug Risner and Walter Edwards for advice and encouragement. Daniel Meyer-Dinkgräfe has been incredibly patient and supportive as an editor. Special thanks to my husband, Richard Haley, who has been my constant companion through this trek.

Prologue

Dream/Archive: The Australian Central Desert as Generative Environment

After spending several weeks in the sands of the Todd-Mparntwe Riverbed in Alice Springs, Northern Territory, Australia, I came home to receive the semi-arid hills in Fairfield, in the Central Valley of California, as camel humps – precious, personified and dear to me in a way I had never experienced before. One year later, after a week of performing in the crisp dirt and rocky underground of the desert location of Wendover, Utah, I returned again to my native California to receive the foothills of Merced outside of Yosemite National Park as intimate acquaintances. I could see their gentle vastness as I never had before. I was no longer alienated from them as enemies, with the perspective of a kid raised on the coast and fearful of any sort of loathsome dryness.

My experiences in the desert had somehow brought me closer to my own home territory by alienating me from my pre-existing frame of reception of these environments. These changes, which I have observed to represent sustained cognitive transformations, are the reason I have become invested in durational site-based performance projects in misunderstood spaces, middle-of-nowheres, those locations that American West writer Wallace Stegner refers to as "the romantic waste places of the world" (2003: 321).

While I knew that my perspective had shifted in a dramatic way as a result of these performances in desert spaces, and was marked by a shift in both the language I used to describe these spaces and the feeling state I now associated with arid locations, I did not yet understand just why the change had occurred. Furthermore, it was curious to me that an experience *elsewhere* had changed my reception of *home* – in other words, my experience *there* was informing my understanding and appreciation of *here*.

In both cases, the transformation in my experience of place had gone from rejection and fear of arid climates to respect and admiration, even fondness, for those same locations and others similar. What was the constitution of my resistance to an arid environment in the first place? Was I simply naïve to the diversity of ecologies that the world offers? Or had I been enculturated with a series of metaphorical constructs around desert environments that had, until now, informed my cognitive reception of place?

On Balance as a Site-Specific Mode of Thinking

My experience and thinking about the desert have been shaped to a large degree by work with choreographer Tess de Quincey, and her BodyWeather[1] performance group De Quincey Company, who made a series of journeys to the Northern Territory between 1999-2005 for the purposes of research and creative activity. I was with the De Quincey Company (DQCo.) on their 2005 journey to Alice Springs, Northern Territory, during which time they re-hearsed and performed their production of *Dictionary of Atmospheres* as part of the Alice Desert Festival. I was an observer, an intern, a publicity person and social-secretary of sorts, and a part of the production crew that stomped around in the sands of the Todd-Mparntwe Riverbed supporting the perfor-mance with lights and props and technology.

As I charted the means by which DQCo. engaged with the environment, I could not help but chart my personal reaction to the space. In our first site visits to the riverbed and adjacent Spencer Hill, all part of the kilometer of space that we would traverse as part of the performance, I was particularly aware of sensations of being off-balance. There were distinct differences in my physical experience that produced these sensations: a stronger sense of gravitational pull on climbing Spencer Hill, an inability to effectively navi-gate the thick riverbed sands with my inexperienced feet. And there were

---

[1] "BODYWEATHER is a broadbased training that proposes a practical strategy to the mind and to the body. It is not just for 'professional dancers' or 'performance practi-tioners' alone but is an open investigation that can be relevant for anyone interested in exploring the body. The term and philosophical basis for BODYWEATHER was founded by butoh dancer Min Tanaka and his MAI-JUKU PERFORMANCE COM-PANY, Japan. Drawing from both eastern and western dance, sports training, martial arts and theatre practice, it is a ground training that develops a conscious relation devoid of any specific aesthetic. As a former member of Mai-Juku 1985-91, Tess de Quincey introduced the BODYWEATHER philosophy and methodology into Aus-tralia in 1989. BODYWEATHER is the basis of her practice as a performer and cho-reographer" ("About BodyWeather"). I will use "BodyWeather" throughout this manuscript, but will preserve different manifestations of the word (e.g. Bodyweather) when quoting others' writing.

also emotional sensations of being off-balance tied to the physical reality of place: my fear of the sun, my fear of and attempts to engage with the feral dogs that roamed in packs around the performance space and in the town.

I was discombobulated in any number of ways and employed various strategies to protect and tend to myself, which manifested in the sometimes neurotic application of sunblock and insistence on wearing many layers of clothing regardless of how hot it became. One evening after dusk, as we were wrapping up rehearsal, a company member had to remind me to take off the straw hat that I had been wearing all day. And though the sun was long gone, taking with it the function of my hat, the thought of exposing my head to the night air after being wrapped up for so many hours felt … unnatural. Without that brim, pulling my gaze down and in, it felt as if my crown might just disappear into the dark unknown of the big sky.

These kinds of being off-balance at first were quite alright. I accepted that I trailed behind everyone as we walked the riverbed and I conscientiously found a poetry of exploration between foot and sand. As days passed, however, I devised a plan to resist gravity, sand, and imbalance. The De Quincey Company is enchanted by efficiency, and I started to feel that my imbalance was not efficient. Noting that the Alice Springs high school cross country team used the riverbed for training, I started to jog out towards the performance site in the mornings to better acquaint myself with the sand. My endurance increased on each run, and soon I learned how to triumph over my own turtle's pace, practicing sprinting across the riverbed throughout the day.

While most of what I am describing does not constitute what would be considered the "formal" part of De Quincey training, which is based in Japanese BodyWeather technique, these everyday elements illustrate the complex nature of participating in a DQCo. production process. While on site in Alice, training to "be-in-place" involved an integration of daily life activities – walking to the rehearsal space, buying necessary items at the supermarket, distributing publicity at the vegetarian Laksa restaurant where we liked to eat. And so the training "technique", when in production mode, encompasses the totality of all of our experiences on-site.

Cultivating a sense of balance that is specific to each performance technique reflects the aesthetics of production as well as the embodied philosophy underlying the form. Developing a university movement curriculum for actors, Barbara Sellers-Young has observed that each student's sense of balance, while entirely individual, is informed and constructed through an interplay between environmental and cultural stimuli:

> [A]s toddlers, we learn the concept of "balance" as we investigate sitting, then crawling, then walking, and other forms of locomotion. But as we learn balance through walking, we also engage, through imitation, with previously established cultural codes that teach specific "modes of thinking" concerning concepts such as balance. This fusing of movement and cultural codes creates distinctive conceptual meanings for the individual, concepts elaborated upon as we experience a variety of somatic states. (1998: 181)

Sellers-Young's words reveal the way in which balance is at once conceptual, physiological and ecological.

The process of renegotiating my sense of balance in the sand stood in for my process of finding a sense of balance in this unfamiliar environment. In this way, conceptually, space came to become place by virtue of my developing relationship to the details of the ecological environment. The sand became a character in my experience, a scene partner. The physical experience of finding balance in the sand conceptually transformed generic details of space into the intimacy of place. Place-based artist Jane Quon summarizes the distinction between space and place and suggests the qualitative implications for each category:

> Scholars of place differentiate 'place' from 'space' in a way that endows 'place' with a value that is withheld from 'space'. 'Space' is transformed into 'place' by the human investment of meaning upon a geographical tract. 'Place' is boundaried; 'space' is amorphous, featureless, unshaped. 'Place' is identified in accordance with characteristics said to inhere within its boundaries. 'Space' is devoid of identifying marks and characteristics. (2004: 1)

My experience of place, while working with the De Quincey Company, is indicative of the way that, in site-based practices, conceptual thinking, and the language that we use to explain our conceptual thinking, is not only embodied but en-grounded. DQCo.'s longitudinal creative work in the Northern Territory is engaged in a practice of ecological philosophy, developing a core set of metaphoric re-constructions of the Australian Central Desert through embodied experiences of place.

Metaphors in Body and in Ground

De Quincey Co. is a dance company, but also highly involved with how oral and written language is conceived, uttered and documented in relation to the translation and preservation of the choreography that they build, which is all improvisationally-based. Language – both physical language and spoken and written language – is constantly generated in the rehearsal room, fastidiously produced and reproduced in group conversations, and then transferred to personal notebooks, dry erase boards, computer charts and diagrams. During my observations of their rehearsal process for *Dictionary of Atmospheres*, documents and documentation materials were literally everywhere throughout the generative process. It was not uncommon to have various packets of paper with source material and emerging and revised descriptions of movement phrases photocopied several times in a given week and distributed to all of the core participants.

This is part of how the Company makes work. A substantial amount of rehearsal time is devoted to languaging each piece of choreography (creating oral and written language associated with movements, gestures, phrases and episodes within the choreography) and then situating those descriptions in relation to everything else built. This process is also potentially informed by an awareness that the work is being archived, as many of Tess' projects are long-term and built in affiliation with the University of Sydney's Department of Performance Studies.

When I go back over all of the documentation that I collected during my observations of the rehearsal and performances of *Dictionary of Atmospheres*, what I notice are a series of metaphors that the company has developed over time that are informed by and are inextricably connected to the Central Desert. These metaphorical structures are part of the means by which the company makes work, informing the way the choreography looks as well as the way that it lives in the performance space. These structures are also constitutive of philosophical perspectives that represent the way that the company – and in this instance, I define DQCo. in terms of its collective base of participants and collaborators spanning the years 1999-2005 – has interpreted and responded to the Central Desert locations of Hamilton Downs and Alice Springs.

These metaphors are part of the company's metapragmatic system – those linguistic structures that the company uses to create work as well as to describe and explain their work. They are unique to this particular working environment in the way that they are used and the deep philosophical significance and implications that they have for an individual and cultural reception of place. The DQCo. investigations in Alice and Hamilton Downs, examined over time, illustrate how company members, individually and collectively, have endeavored to construct new metaphorical frameworks for engagement in and relationship to these locations as outsiders[2].

Within the literature on performance and cognition (see, for instance, McConachie and Hart 2006; Saltz 2007; Blair 2008; McConachie 2008), particularly those works focused on the relationship between cognitive science and linguistics (see, for instance, Blair and Lutterbie 2011), there is room for further consideration of the ecological contributions to performers' cognitive development. Site-based performance practice affords us the opportunity to invest these discourses on performance and cognition with an environmental consideration. This environmental consideration, which I am referring to as an "engrounded" consideration, is characterized by an attention to the history of human encounters with a specific ecological environment, examining the ways in which the land, itself, contributes to philosophies and methodologies of being-in-place.

Particularly because of the durational nature of DQCo.'s site-based work, the Company's performance practices provide a microcosm within which to investigate George Lakoff and Mark Johnson's concept of metaphor. Lakoff and Johnson, in the key texts *Metaphors We Live By* (1980) and *Philosophy in the Flesh* (1999), theorize that foundational Western thinking is rooted in core metaphors that describe what we feel in our bodies and act out in our behavior, exemplified by familiar phrases such as "man vs. nature" and "nature as human agent." Site-based performance practice facilitates the development of new metaphoric constructions of place that are not only located in the individual's body (embodied), but also located in a specific place (engrounded).

Elemental Form and Metaphoric Function in *Dictionary of Atmospheres*

The metaphoric structures that De Quincey Company have created are both embodied and engrounded and are designed to offer a challenge to what they

---

[2] I use the term "outsiders" here to indicate that Company members are neither from the Central Desert originally, nor do they currently live in the Central Desert. Most Company members, as well as most participants in De Quincey's workshops in the Central Desert, 1999-2005, live in Sydney or Melbourne.

consider to be damaging historical constructions of the human relationship to environment. The DQCo. metaphors, which are elemental in nature, functioned to generate performance work in *Dictionary of Atmospheres* – they also serve to assist Company members in developing a radically restorative relationship to the Central Desert environment.

One of the central metaphors associated with the training, rehearsal and performance process for *Dictionary of Atmospheres* is "Body as Conduit." Body-as-Conduit refers to the way that work is cultivated, generated and shared and the way that meaning is created in that environment. While the results of the Company's investigation of body-as-conduit manifested in a single week of performances in Alice Springs in 2005, this particular metaphor must be understood as the product of decades of collective investigation among participants in Tess' work. De Quincey's work in the Central Desert, including the TripleAlice laboratories (1999-2001), which brought international groups of artists, historians, scholars and other cultural workers to Hamilton Downs, just outside of Alice Springs, is the most notable influence on *Dictionary of Atmospheres*. But her work at Lake Mungo in New South Wales (1991-94) and numerous other site-specific projects in both rural and urban locations can be understood as exerting a cumulative influence on what was created in *Dictionary of Atmospheres*.

In the TripleAlice laboratories and other BodyWeather workshops, Tess provides mechanisms for individual and group work in devised performance. One such mechanism is called an "invitation," in which participants attempt to identify with a certain element in the ecological environment. Gay McAuley, writing about the TripleAlice experience, describes participants' exploration of the environs as such:

> The most powerful of all, from the perspective of performers and observers, were the exercises in which the performers observed intensively an element of the natural world around them (a cloud, a rock, even a blade of grass) and, through this concentrated attention, attempted (as de Quincey described it later) to empathise on a cellular level with the chosen element. (2000: 4-5)

As individuals, participants in De Quincey's workshops, rehearsals, and generative sessions create a relationship with a particular element and then share that experience, performatively, with the rest of the company.

This process of invitation became part of the way that *Dictionary of Atmospheres* was actually built. Invitations at the Triple Alice laboratories and workshops were recorded in the video footage, journals and ethnographic notebooks connected with the tenure of investigation and archived at the University of Sydney's Department of Performance Studies. When the development for *Dictionary of Atmospheres* began, some of the most resonant invitations were then resuscitated and found-again as the company went into the formal process of workshopping and rehearsing in the months leading up to the performances in Alice Springs. The individual embodied experiences of place that had been created and archived in the invitation process were then translated to the performers – some of whom has been a part of the Triple Alice experiences, and some of whom had not.

"Invitation" as a generative mechanism operates throughout the DQCo. creative process, spanning many years, from the beginning work of an individual creating a relationship to a single element of the ecological environment to the work of translation of that experience to the company performing *Dictionary of Atmospheres*. In each stage of development, the body of the individual and the body of the company as a collective *conducts* experiential, site-based information and allows it to pass through them as performance. This manifests in actual, literal choreographic "bodies" that conduct the energy of place: for instance – for the *Dictionary of Atmospheres* production, performers explored collective improvisations around the ideas of "smoke body," "shadow body," and "storm body". While the idea of a performer's body as being a conduit (for energy, for character, for choreographic phrasing) is arguably a familiar metaphoric structure used in a variety of performance training contexts, for De Quincey Company, "body as conduit" is unique in that it is always a reference to the body's relationship to the specificities of site – an attempt to channel the energy of place.

"Body as conduit" – a conceptual framework for the making of performance as well as the thinking about the form and function of performance – is derived from the Company's perceptions of the conductivity of desert sand. De Quincey Company is overtly interested in the elemental composition of sand as quartz and silica and its properties of translucence and conductivity *as* forms of intelligence. These elemental properties of sand feature prominently in their archival documents and documentation for *Dictionary of Atmospheres* as "underlying energetics", or, those embodied philosophical concepts that inform the piece while also expressing the history of encounters with the Central Desert as place. De Quincey has, through engrounded metaphoric structures like "body as conduit", created a metalinguistic structure of making work and theorizing the work based on the actual elements (i.e. sand, wind, atmosphere) in which she is working. In this sense, the objective underlying *Dictionary of Atmospheres* is to create an energetic relationship to the land without trying to replicate the mythological or spiritual system of the people of the land. It's about creating one's own relationship, one's own dynamic with the land, which Tess cooks down to "keeping the place alive" as a "dreaming body" (De Quincey 2005).

What makes the De Quincey Company's work unique among site-based performance endeavors is the type of presence that they are trying to establish through this relationship to place. De Quincey's creative process leading up to *Dictionary of Atmospheres* sets up repeated periods of itinerant residencies in the desert spaces in and around Alice Springs. This performance presence asks what it means to wander conscientiously in a place repeatedly over many years' time, and what is at stake in uncovering one's relationship to that place through wandering. This process thus aims to confront, in its approach and creative methodology, historical projects of colonialism, imperialism and expansion in the Australian Central Desert and the immense loss and grief that has accompanied those projects. Gay McAuley writes of the social and cultural implications of such a process:

> When performance engages deeply with its chosen site, it brings up ideas of place, history and memory, and it has the potential to disrupt, disturb, and even to change the way people see the familiar surroundings of their daily lives ... Tess De Quincey's laboratory raises questions about the ways in which performers experience place and what they do with that experience, and these questions are profoundly important at a time when the impact of human beings on the environment is subjecting the entire planet to massive stress. (2000: 2, 7)

De Quincey's journeys to the Center also retrace the actual paths of migration taken by colonizers from the coastal periphery to the center of the Australian continent – historical paths taken in the European "unsettlement" (Tompkins 2006)[3] of the continent and the routes still taken by the majority of visitors to the Northern Territory, who live on the concentrated strip that is the geographical (coastal) fringe but the economic and "cultural" center of the nation.

---

[3] For Tompkins, "unsettlement" describes the histories of displacement related to the British occupation of Australia and the related "*uncertainties* of Australian spatiality that dominate on the stage" (42).

De Quincey's work in the Central Desert is unique in the information that it produces because of the presence that it establishes, but also because of the specific ecology that it investigates. What Tess has contributed is a method of performance-making-in-residence that is thorough enough and durational enough to allow us to witness the effects of the environment on a group of performers' conscious experience of place.

As performers find their balance on uneven ground, they are challenging their existing embodied construction of balance. They are, as Sellers-Young writes, elaborating on their existing conceptual framework by taking themselves into various somatic states related to a specific ecology. On a larger scale, this type of work is conscientious about restoring perceived imbalances in the history of human engagement with the ecological environment. In this way, De Quincey's site-based performance practice invests the discourse on performance training and cognition with an environmental consideration.

Site-Based Performance as Ecological Thinking – Embodied Language of Restoration

The complexity and immense value of studying site-based performance is that it is subject to all of the elements of traditional performance, which is often, by virtue of the space in which it is performed, circumscribed or built on the illusion of circumscription. With Tess' work, there is a conscientious effort towards including more information about the environmental location. The point *is* the location, with the performative efforts existing in order to direct audience focus towards elements of the site – the topography of the landscape, the setting sun, a sacred space – and towards the collective response of the performers over time to these elements in their embodied choreographic interpretation of the country.

De Quincey Company aims to develop a greater consciousness around experiencing the land. Each performer may be drawn to the land for different reasons and called to do work that looks and feels very different. But what is undeniable in any of these cases is that the land traces itself onto performers' understanding of their bodies and their relationship to place. DQCo. training is thus training to be-in-place. The *Dictionary of Atmospheres* installation of the Company as an "atmospheric presence" in the landscape invited performers to receive information from the ecological environment. This information in performance encourages performers and audience members alike to reconsider how existing acts and policies towards the environment reflect the legacy of cultural metaphoric constructs like "nature as human agent."

Site-based dance that is durationally and intentionally engaged with the ecological information of place involves a process of cultivating a creative relationship to environment that produces new linguistic metaphors but also, with each chorographic phrase, its own embodied metaphor. The performances are expressing the metaphoric philosophy of place and metaphoric representation of place. De Quincey's linguistically generative methodology – the process wherein Tess and company members produce spoken and written language that accounts for, describes, and places all choreographic information in performance – is a step between experience and metaphor.

If the objective of this particular site-based dance is to create a restorative relationship to nature, then perhaps DQCo. has endeavored to reposition the environment as teacher. In my experience working with De Quincey Co. on *Dictionary of Atmospheres*, I must consider that my revised experience and conceptual framing of balance was not merely based on my choice to negotiate the sand. I would rather contend that it was about the sand teaching me something about place and my role in that place – in terms of survival, in terms of cohabitation, in terms of philosophy.

In *Dictionary of Atmospheres*, the Company endeavored to imagine the land as speaking through them. This objective is a response to the premise that humans historically have developed a variety of tactics to navigate ecological challenges to human authority, resisting the lessons that the land offers. But, for DQCo., the presence of the land is undeniable. It waits for us. And if we linger long enough and return often enough, we may come to receive information that transforms us. We may come to find a restorative relationship to the existing philosophical framework of ancestors who broke through the surface of the earth.

Lakoff and Johnson's argument for embodied philosophy calls for an abandonment of disembodied reasoning in favor of an "empirically responsible" discourse on thought, word and deed (1999: 3). Philosopher Lorraine Code's argument for "ecological thinking" calls for a revision of the conventional human engagement with knowledge in favor of "enact[ing] principles of ideal cohabitation" (2006: 24). Code reminds us of the complex implications of adopting a policy of ecological thinking:

> [E]cological thinking is not simply thinking *about* ecology or *about* the environment: it generates revisioned modes of engagement with knowledge, subjectivity, politics, ethics, science, citi-

> zenship, and agency, which pervade and reconfigure theory and
> practice alike. First and foremost a thoughtful practice, thinking
> ecologically carries with it a large measure of responsibility – to
> know somehow more *carefully* than single surface readings can
> allow. (2006: 24)

Tess De Quincey's multi-year project in and around Alice Springs is an example of ecological thinking in practice: practical philosophy that is embodied and engrounded. The very notion of a "surface reading" is opened up and turned over when considered in the context of the real time and history of De Quincey's return migration back, to the same place, to the same surfaces, to the same sands, to find balance again. The practice, in this case, significantly complicates and deepens the theory. Neurophysiologist Semir Zeki (1999) contends that the creative process is an outward manifestation of the brain's search for constancies in an ever-changing environment, something "created by the brain to extend its own reach in the task" (Freeman 2003: 217). "Art practice as conveyance" as a metaphoric construct illustrates only a fraction of performance's creative function. In terms of ecological thinking, site-based performance is perhaps "art practice as purveyance," in keeping with literary scholar Eric Wilson's prescription:

> [I]f one wishes to forge a living (*ecological*) relationship to nature
> – as opposed to a deathly (*exploitative or pastoral*) one – then one
> will engage in practices that vouchsafe two results: *participation*
> in the processes of life and *purveyance* of these processes for the
> edification of others. (2000: 26)

Dictionary as Archive: The Presence of Words

This book charts my own personal process of understanding *Dictionary* of *Atmospheres*: a performance that occurred in Alice Springs in 2005 with Tess De Quincey and a host of collaborators; a performance that was days in the happening, weeks in the setting up, months in the rehearsing, and years in the making, the writing, the dreaming. Accordingly, this is a book attempting to archive an archive of an archive. And the sentence just uttered allows us to begin to consider the flexibility of that very word – *archive* – as a verb and then a noun and then a noun once again, but this time different. I return to the big blue book of words on my desk (the dictionary) to rediscover where *archive* might take me this time in function and etymology. And I am reminded that an archive may be: an individual document or record; a collection of related data sets organized around guideposts like family, institution, idea; the physical structure containing the matter; the act of collecting, organizing, retrieving these memory capsules.

My reflections on the performance-making processes involved with *Dictionary of Atmospheres* as I experienced them and as I've hoped to share them with others have sent me back time and again to the little details of words and the larger themes to which these details allude and from which these details elude. There's a concomitant attraction and repulsion that keeps me coming back to the need for words and the escape from words. So we have archive, reminding us of its flexibility as a piece of text. But even as it insists on its adaptive potential, I'm having an intuitive, embodied response you might call subtext or connotation – that *the* archive and *to* archive suggests a form of containment – a management, attempt at control or domination of information that implies something ultimate, a containment that seems disingenuous if not downright dishonest. And then I find a way through the debacle: Tess' work is inherently archival because it cleverly resists containment in its own meticulous process of containing.

An example of Tess' archival work: *Dictionary of Atmospheres* has its own webpage describing itself. The text was created before the piece was staged in Alice, was circulated via electronic and paper trails during and throughout the creative process, and will exist circulating in these media for years after the performance is "over". At the moment, it is an electronic post-it note and a cyber-effigy, a tacked up pin-up and an homage, in one spot and everywhere for remembering and rediscovering. The bits of text that serve the particularly paradoxical archival role that I've mentioned are here on the website: *to wander, to drift, to transform, to rove, to meander, to reflect.* Each verb, placed to tantalize and draw in – in essence, to capture – is nonetheless an embrace of the nebulous, an invitation to the in-between. The language suggests what was hoped to happen – after all, it was written prior to the ultimate landing in Alice for the showing in 2005 – but also marks what did happen. The piece took place before, during and after the gloaming, the magic hour – charting and responding to the transition and transformation between daytime and nighttime. And my mind moves towards dreams. A logic of dreaming that might inform the relationship between this performance archive and the act of writing presently.

Archive as Dream: Writing Presently

Why a logic of dreaming? The language, itself, implies the dream state – be it the state of waking dream or REM cycle dream – it implies the continuous dream made up of the juxtaposition of the everyday and the extraordinary that characterizes our anytime experience. And then there is the time factor – that if we are attuned to our circadian rhythms, the gradual shift to darkness is a natural, environmental invitation to submit to being closed-eyed and dreaming. And most importantly, the archive as the dream just seems to make sense. The archive is what we hope it will be, what we predict it will be, what we imagine it will be and, at the end of the day, an otherwise random conglomeration of bits that we've decided make sense together, tell a story together. And this is the stuff of dreams. An archive whose structure permits the "real" to act as a gateway to the magical, a space where the weird may be weird but not *wrong*. The archive as dream allows for an alternative presence in the creative science of performance making and performance documentation.

This type of writing presently is evident in what we see from Tim Etchells' *Certain Fragments* (1999) or his generous weblog documentation of Forced Entertainment's rehearsal processes. From 27 May 2006, Etchells translates a waking dream also known as rehearsal:

> Wendy dancing with a plastic sword. Or in cave-gear and sunglasses. Dancing right next to Jerry. Pushing as close to him as she can without touching him, as he stands there motionless. This thing about bodies. Example-bodies. One standing still, flat, the other in constant motion, twisting and turning in three dimensions. As if to say – these two things are possible. Movement and stillness. (Etchells 2006)

His words are memoir and autobiography, biography of the show, novel and ethnographic fieldnote. They are a gesture at getting not so much in-between experience, but getting along, moving along in an environment of memory production and reflection: the creation of a passage in a storm of information, the laying of a possible path.

These gestures resonate strongly with Victor Turner's concept of liminality (1974) in all its implications – cultural information produced with a recognition of its own embedded contestation. And yet these gestures are not *about* the conflict between the production of meaning and its contestations. Instead, these traces, these inscriptions are created perhaps *despite* and in addition to this conflict. This type of writing presence – a kind of dream archive – knows that it cannot contain and has an interest in resisting containment. Language in this environment acts as a vehicle, a means of transportation from site to site, between ideas, amidst events.

Dance anthropologist Sally Ann Ness delves into the dilemma regarding language in durational performance documentation, explaining of her ethnographic notes: "They are not my memories intact. They are keeping my memories from dying" (1996: 129). For Ness, the write-up does not contain the memorial topography – instead, it is merely a channel through which memory is resurrected and born again and again. Her requisite response becomes one of resistance to the inherent containment of ethnographic practice:

> My task: A text that breaks with the logic of the ethnographic corporation, in this case by *telling* something "'way too soon." A text that writes against the separation of the ethnography and the memoir, a text written between author and fieldnote-maker, the fallible, inconsistent, imaginative individual who existed when the notes were written down, who has since outgrown herself, but who is also an outgrowth of the earlier figure, who maintains a limited substantive continuity as an organism and as a form of memory. (Ness 1996: 129-30)

The paradox of this process of charting, of archiving, is the inescapable presence of absence. With this in mind, my turning to the dream state is not simply an admission of absence – nor is it an out wherein we're forgiven our inadequacies as collectors. It's simply a different rhetorical strategy that wants to take on more information, include more ambiguity, admit to being within the self in the interest of more possible data.

Jacques Derrida and Hélène Cixous deal directly with the phenomenon of the dream as the archive. In *Dream I Tell You* (2006), Cixous has collected 50 of her dreams written down over the past two decades and organized them as a narrative to Derrida, himself. Derrida's *Geneses, Genealogies, Genres, and Genius* (2006) is a response and valuation (though not interpretation, to my knowledge) of Cixous' contribution to theory through a form of poetic reasoning he finds significantly feminine. Cixous' writing is a merging between thought, response and doing, an integration of imagination and self:

> Dreams are theatres which put on the appearance of a play in order to slip other unavowable plays between the lines of the avowal scenes: you reader-spectator are aware of this but you forget what you know so you can be charmed and taken in. You connive with you own trickery. You pull the wool over your eyes. The thinner than a razor blade that slips between you and yourself is an imperceptible vertical hyphen. You are a you [Tu es un tu]. Do you see what I mean? Who is you? I am reminding you of the dream's delicate work; first it slips the invisible laser scalpel between the letters: t, u, t'es eu, tu, [you've been had] next between the signifieds Siamese twinned by homonymy: tu es tu [you are you] that's why, etant tu [being you/having remained silent] tu ne peux plus te taire [you can no longer remain silent]. As for the bistouri [scalpel], il bisse tout ris [repeats, echoes, all laughter]. (2006: 4)

She's playing with metaphors, relying on metaphors, and, in the process, revealing the poetics of thought and alluding to the magic of thought, the magic of thinking, the magic of performance-making: ineffable, out of reach, seductive, but nonetheless present, real – something tangible even if novel. Derrida's description of Cixous' narration of her nocturnal journeys could just as easily be describing attempts at articulating the intricate immensities of a performance process. Derrida refers to Cixous' work as a "translation of the infinite world" (2006: 24).

Another example of an archive from *Dictionary of Atmospheres*: We are in a meeting with Tess and her collaborators discussing ideas for a 72-hour performance, tentatively titled *Pivotal Country*, which would be a longer durational project planned for some future date, and for which *Dictionary of Atmospheres* may serve as a kind of a gateway or first draft. I have arrived about half way through the conversation and one of Tess' collaborators, musician Jim Denley, has brought up the fact that the part of the Todd-Mparntwe Riverbed where *Dictionary of Atmospheres* is currently being performed and where the 72-hour piece would be hosted is an actual bed for the people who live there. Permanent and semi-permanent squatters set up makeshift campsites in the riverbed, which is dry for 95% of the year. Different members of the discussion contribute and a few minutes later Tess says "I understand this space as a transient space….I would like to try to sleep there and find out if that's actually ok. What my body says is you've gotta feel it. You've gotta feel your way." The conversation continues and a bit later, Russell asks if the 72 hour performance would be *about being awake*. "The lovely thing", says Tess, "is when people just sit there and fall asleep and you're performing for five sleeping bodies" (de Quincey 2005).

This writing project follows a desire for words that suggest the dream/archive dynamic set up in the DeQCo. process. And in that statement, I am attempting to mindfully incorporate a self-reflexive admittance of my inherent inability to capture this very dynamism in all of its sensible randomness, all of its logical incoherence. Writes Allan Hobson of the intertwined narrative and neurological mysteries of dreaming:

> While sleep persists, our brains are more active in dreams than in some states of waking – one of the many paradoxes uncovered by modern sleep science. But I would call attention not only to this heightened intensity but also to the increase in the variety of forms that one may perceive during the dream state. Some contemporary psychologists claim that dream mentation is not uniquely bizarre since waking fantasy may contain all the elements present in dreams. But dreams put these bizarre elements together with a convincing reality, a pictorial clarity, sometimes even an artistic talent that are difficult for most of us to achieve in the waking state. It is this hyperreal quality, with mutually incompatible, bizarre elements effortlessly combined, to which I apply the term *autocreative*. These most extraordinary dream "tableaux" are made by the sleeping brain-mind without access to external cues; the composition uses only the traces of experience that are stored in memory. (1988: 17)

Hobson lays out a theory of reciprocal interaction wherein physiological processes, memory and imagination mediate, react and respond to each other in the dream state, producing "autocreative" picture-stories with seemingly random origins that are translated into narratives imbued with their own "hyperreal" logic and meaning. Thus, for Hobton, memory, as the cumulative and ever-changing archive living in relative states of accessibility, in the dream state serves to receive atmospheric information and ground it in the established network of data in the dreamer's "brain-mind," as he describes it. The components of the ordinary dreamer's atmosphere: the stomach's chemistry, the lopsided bed, the ticking clock are potentially the lightning bolts of data received through memory and made meaningful, made narrative, by virtue of their connection to cumulative embodied knowledge as memory.

My proposal is that the components of the *Dictionary of Atmospheres* environment: the sands of the riverbed, the colors of the sky at sunset, the boulders between mountain crevices are the lightning bolts of data received through the DQCo. team's dream-like somatic experience and made meaningful, made narrative by virtue of their connection to the Company's archives of investigation into the country around Alice, around Hamilton Downs, in the Northern Territory.

The objective with *Dictionary of Atmospheres* is to create an energetic relationship to the land without trying to replicate or even comment specifically upon the mythological or spiritual system of the people of the land. It's about creating one's own relationship, one's own dynamic with the land, which Tess cooks down to "keeping the place alive" as a "dreaming body". Says Tess, "in effect, we're trying to create our own dreamings ... We need enough openness for interpretation" (de Quincey 2005).

Over the period 1999-2005, director/choreographer Tess de Quincey and a team of international artists conducted a series of art-laboratories and performances in and around the town of Alice Springs, Northern Territory in affiliation with the University of Sydney's Department of Performance Studies. These art-labs culminated in the 2005 performance of *Dictionary of Atmospheres*, which was staged during the Alice Desert Festival. In the chapters that follow, I will combine reflections from my own practice-based research, conducted while interning with de Quincey July-September 2005, with analysis of ethnographic fieldnotes, participant journals, and archival research from all three of the Triple Alice art labs. I do this work as a means of exploring the De Quincey Company's approach to and articulation of place. Desert places, in these explorations, emerge as a set of useful problems, or, valuable paradoxes that exert an inadvertent aesthetic presence in the group's work. Chapters are organized in a reverse chronology. Starting with analysis of an initial "problem moment" that I observed in the 2005 production of *Dictionary of Atmospheres* (chapter 1), I then work backwards from that moment to investigate the way that *Dictionary of Atmospheres* was the product of its small regional festival environment (chapter 2), as well as a product of the Triple Alice art- labs which preceded it (chapter 3). In the epilogue, I reflect on the challenge of writing up processes of performance-as-research over time, in light of the eight years that have passed since my encounter with the De Quincey Company.

The desert sites examined in this study consistently reveal themselves, in performance, to be dynamic and even unruly scene partners in the dramas that transpire upon their surfaces. In this sense, these specific sites resist the containment that performance-makers tend to impose upon them in performance. In the performances examined in this study – which range from the formal productions of *Dictionary of Atmospheres* to the semi-formal performances associated with rehearsal environments and art laboratories to the rather informal performances of everyday life that occur in and around these more structured interactions – a kind of "feral" consciousness emerges as a dialogue between the artists and places engaged, revealing, among other things, participants' complex feelings of tension and displacement associated with the history of British unsettlement of the land, colonialism, and its aftermath.

This work is essentially a long-form essay in which I meditate on a handful of moments that I observed July-September 2005 which have simultaneously puzzled and intrigued me. The significance of working backwards in time – starting with those performance moments in 2005 and then drawing together threads, texts and thoughts from the rehearsals and art-laboratories that preceded them – lies in an interest in creating an intentionally meandering, nomadic account which walks backwards both as a means to unravel the deep impact that the experience has had on me, and as well as a means to investigate where this experience came from, what informed it, what cultural practices it was derived from, and why it is of value as a "problem-idea". To this extent, this writing is always partial, fragmentary and inconclusive by design, an "open book" (Pollock 1999: 23) which is only suggestive and delivered in the spirit of a self that is, in fact, a "mess of errors" (Pollock 2007: 247). A modest offering at best, I hope that this work is read as a search for understanding of the "divine imperturbability" of the desert (Tuan 2001: 16) and the performance-makers who are attracted to it.

Chapter One

Dream Disrupted: Figuring the Displaced Thing in *Dictionary of Atmospheres*

The host environment may be altered irrevocably by the presence of a new organism but so too, inevitably, is the one who runs wild transformed by the terrain in which it insinuates itself … The feral animal or plant, in this sense, figures for the entirety of objects, practices, and techniques that were uplifted from metropolitan centres of the northern hemisphere and 'unleashed' at the colonial periphery.

— Nigel Clark (2003: 166)

You have to be willing to make a big mistake because it leads somewhere.

— Peter Sellars (2002: 138)

On four gentle September evenings in 2005, a crowd of forty or so gathered on the sands of the dry Todd-Mparntwe riverbed in Alice Springs, Northern Territory. The meeting place had been established by the De Quincey Company, a group of performers based in Sydney who were the invited guests of the Alice Desert Festival. Over the course of an hour's time, the audience – composed primarily of the town's residents, with a few visitors from here and there in Australia and abroad – was led on a walking tour through the thick, coarse sands of the riverbed. They were guided by five energetic dancers dressed in clothing saturated in the dust of the environment, a wandering saxophonist who breathed strange gurgles and gulps into his instrument, and a production crew toting an array of properties, boom boxes, set pieces and lighting equipment.

By the time the experience was nearly over, audience members had seen all manner of human movement. At the outset of the piece, a male dancer, leaf in mouth, held a draped pose across the trunk of a tree with such stillness that it required sometimes one or two takes to recognize that he was there. Midway through the piece, the five dancers executed acrobatic feats, kicking up a cloud of dust as one woman pulled another's hair, one man bit a woman's leg. The implements provided by the production crew rendered a scene in which the dancers wrapped and trapped the audience in 50 meters of yellow caution tape, only to abandon the entangled audience and take off running towards three enormous video projection screens made of PVC pipe and shadecloth.

By the second-to-last scene, the sun's light had disappeared completely and now the primary illumination remaining was the reflection of the abstract imagery projected on the shadecloth screens. Two female dancers, wearing translucent colored plastic raincoats backwards, carried giant sculpted bundles of the tumbleweed-like plant spinifex on a slow march through the sand. In the minimal light, only shadows and highlights suggested the women's presence, the projection reflections itinerantly picking up the space between the darkness of each woman's body and the edges of the stiff, translucent raincoats. They were the living disguised as ghosts, and the spinifex they carried was similarly between worlds.

A wild, prickly plant that populates over 25 percent of the Central Desert landscape (Allan and Southgate 2002: 146), spinifex can be a hearty, sturdy nuisance that pops up through the sands and gets stuck in boots and scratches arms and can't be picked entirely out of clothing. Here, now, in the arms of the women, it lay dormant as a dead child – pulled from the earth where it grew 60 kilometers away from the performance site, wrestled and stuffed into vehicles, and then tamed into tidy bundles held together with twine.[1] The taming concealed the identity of the spinifex, which continued to assert itself only at the edges of the bundles, where the scratchy, scraggly tips of the plant defied the organization of the binding. Cutting a horizontal path that bisected the earlier choreographic journey through the sand, the two women became three, who then lit the spinifex bundles on fire, and disappeared into the darkness.

The audience stood for a moment, and then another. And then one moment more. And then determined that the piece was over. The projections had finished. The spinifex bonfire had finished – its spark and flash proved to be

---

[1] In chapters 2 and 3, I will discuss in detail the process of gathering the spinifex off-site, bringing it back to the performance space, and then preparing the spinifex for performance.

only a momentary phenomenon. The only clear remaining lighting reference was 30 meters in the distance, where 100 flares were lit – far enough away to suggest an end-point that was "backstage space". The audience, who had been guided very specifically for the past hour, who had become expeditiously trained in how to participate in this unusual experience, now found themselves abandoned. The only clear points of reference remaining were memories of events that had already passed. Alone, in the dark, they had come all this way only to be left wondering what to do next. One and two and three at a time, they made their way to the banks of the riverbed in the dark. They, too, disappeared into the darkness.

A reviewer from the Australian arts publication *Real Time* wrote in response to her attendance at the event that "[r]eading unfamiliar movement can be difficult for an audience searching for recognisable forms" and that, while this piece "was not forthcoming" in providing an accessible logic, that "the experience of the desert dusk and the ancient presence of the riverbed" provided for a "spectacular natural stage" (Maher 2005). She was pleased to have simply been in the space. But she, like many others in attendance, were left with a set of uncertainties with regard to how they were *meant* to experience, read and receive the performance. Local reporter Kieran Finnane described both her curiosity with the performance, as well as the limits of her ability to interpret what she saw:

> De Quincey Co were right to recognize the river as the natural theatre of Alice Springs for their performance of Dictionary of Atmospheres. There was a fitting sense of ancient ceremony (that universal need to enact something about our presence on the planet) as people gathered in the river near Schwarz Crescent looking north. Your eye roved the landscape, there was music somewhere, who was playing? There was a tiny group of performers in the distance, what were they doing? Where was this whole event going to take you? The company struggled though, as the performance unfolded, with the sheer scale of their stage. I found my attention only intermittently captured rather than engrossed, though this was also partly to do with the dispersed focus of the whole project – it tried to draw together too many threads. (Finnane 2005)

The De Quincey Company had offered up, in an hour's time, a complex puzzle that challenged even the most seasoned audience members' notions of how to participate in and interpret the semiology of *Dictionary of Atmospheres.*

The confusion that audience members experienced with the piece, as a whole, ranged from a general discontent with the lack of focus-management to direct concern with the ethics of the Company's use of particular images and materials in the riverbed space. These are two separate sorts of problems. On the one hand, site-specific performance is inherently vulnerable to focus-management problems. If audiences do not know where to look, they get anxious about how to look. If audiences do not know how to look and are not affirmed that their not knowing is acceptable – even a good thing – they can become susceptible to individual and collective existential and pragmatic crises that interrupt their ability to comfortably experience the performance.

Site-specific works staged outdoors are exponentially more vulnerable to these types of issues, as practitioners are tasked to factor in the variable ways that the environment will collaborate with sudden changes in light and weather and unexpected contributions from animals and cars and smells and so on. Some performance groups might relish in such environmental disruptions – even devising with these possibilities in mind. While the De Quincey Company was not interested in eschewing these disruptive possibilities by relocating *Dictionary of Atmospheres* in a more contained or containable space, they did not design the performance as an exercise in challenging or disrupting their audiences' reception through *intentional* focus mis-management. In fact, the Company had spent months rehearsing through various contingencies and manners of engaging audiences as a means by which to mitigate some of the confusion that they knew would accompany performing outdoors.

The second type of problem that audiences expressed in their reception of the piece was related to individual and cultural judgments about what sorts of images are appropriate to display and perform in the Todd-Mpartnwe riverbed. Some responses were very specific. Among the images projected on the large shadecloth screens was a video sequence of an Aboriginal woman performing a traditional act that involved rolling hair against her exposed leg. Though the Company had been in consultation with the traditional Aboriginal owners of the site for many months, and though the Company had engaged, from 1999-2005, in the Triple Alice series of cultural exchanges with artists and cultural leaders from Aboriginal communities in the Northern Territory, the use of the imagery reflected an oversight – something that they did not know was inappropriate, something which reflected that the Company was still in the process of learning about Aboriginal cultural values and practices.

Another example of this second type of problem – the ethics of presenting specific sorts of imagery in this space – was the Company's staging of violence. In a sequence that occurred midway through the piece, in which the dancers slapped and spanked each other, pulled on each other's hair, wrestled to the ground and bit one another, certain members of the local audience took offense. In this case, their offense was related to the specific circumstances of the performance site, as the kilometer of riverbed that the Company traversed over the course of *Dictionary of Atmospheres* is a notoriously violent space, in which groups of itinerant Aboriginal people gather, often under the influence of alcohol or petrol. In their article, "Death in a Dry River: Black Life, White Property, Parched Justice", Suvendrini Perera and Joseph Pugliese explain the spatial politics of Alice Springs and situate the marginality of the Todd-Mpartnwe riverbed within that context:

> The contemporary topography of the town and its surrounds is the product of the carving out of cattle stations, missions and reservations from Aboriginal homelands and of a history of forced evacuations, relocations and round-ups ... If Aboriginal people are no longer formally prohibited from remaining within town limits after dark, their places remain on the fringes of Alice Springs: among scattered ceremonial grounds or as presences to be monitored and moved on at the edges of malls and souvenir shops, in dilapidated and dangerous town camps, and in the shadowy, uncertain shelter of the dry river bed. (2011: 66)

Walking through a site in which acts of violence and even murders are not uncommon, some local residents felt that it was careless and unnecessary at least – and perhaps even unethical – for an outside performance group to stage even the suggestion of violence. For the local audience members, it did not matter that the Company had not intended to suggest the *specific* violence that was known to occur in the Todd-Mparntwe riverbed: the knowledge of the violence that occurs regularly in the space informs and haunts the area, exerting an undeniable, palpable presence. And so the fact that the Company's choreography was not even intended to depict violence, per se, but rather a series of intensified physical gestures, was beside the point. The riverbed, as such a highly-charged political and emotional environment, simply could not lend itself to the staging of such an abstract narrative without it becoming an immediate allegorical reference to the very real circumstances of the site and its occupants.

It is important to keep in mind, in this instance, that the *Dictionary of Atmospheres* choreography was created from the movement vocabulary developed during the Triple Alice art labs. Martin Harrison describes the Triple Alice art labs as having:

> no intention to set up a representative 'space' in which the immediacy of locale could, or should, be embodied ... If the experimental practice of the event was definitely locative, *Triple Alice*'s understanding of locus was not, first off, about the representability of place, not about its cultural appropriation and exclusiveness. (2000: 8)

De Quincey's interrogative, experimental approach to site-generated choreography led to the production of movement as a series of perceived "open texts", whereas audience members, walking through this particular site, read these choreographic phrases as "closed texts" (Eco 1984), because the production of meaning around violence is essentially "overdetermined" in this environment (Althusser 2005 [1965]).[2]

The two major types of problems that audiences expressed in response to their attendance at *Dictionary of Atmospheres* can be described on one level as having to do with perceptions of focus-management and cultural insensitivity. And yet, each of these matters is also operating on a second level. The problem with focus-management was more pointedly a problem of audience participation and of the relationship between audience members and performers. The problem with the perceived cultural insensitivity was more pointedly a problem of insensitivity to the specifics of the selected site. At the nexus of these intersecting problems to do with reception lies the Company's use of the plant spinifex. Neither the formal nor the informal reviews of the piece made specific reference to the Company's use of spinifex, or the confusion surrounding the final bonfire. However, the production activities leading up to the spinifex bonfire and the audience behavior following the bonfire represent an emblematic disconnect between the De Quincey Company's intentions for the piece and audiences' reception of the piece.

---

[2] In chapter 3, I will take up a more detailed discussion regarding the paradox of representation in *Dictionary of Atmospheres* as a project created from the choreographic vocabulary developed in the Triple Alice laboratories.

Spinifex, like other materials and imagery mobilized over the course of *Dictionary of Atmospheres*, is culturally loaded. The plant, and particularly the burning of the plant, holds great significance for Aboriginal communities and is also resonant with the history of white settler ignorance of Aboriginal cultural practices. As Phillip A. Clarke (2007: 45) and Allan and Southgate (2002: 145) have articulated, a central aspect of Aboriginal land management across Australia has involved the deliberate firing of vegetation for the purposes of hunting and for the revitalization of flora. Over thousands of years, these practices "shaped the Australian landscape" and "altered the structure of the Australian vegetation" (Clarke 2007: 46). And yet, until very recently, these firing practices have been grossly misinterpreted and undervalued by European settlers, with dangerous consequences (see Rose 1995). To burn spinifex in performance is to invoke ritual and practical Aboriginal firing systems; and it is also an invocation of the histories of white settler ignorance of these systems. It is, further, an invocation of both the histories of European suppression of Aboriginal fire regimes as well as the histories of European tracking of Aboriginal movements *through* their firing practices.

Audience members engaging with *Dictionary of Atmospheres* were, as reviewer Rachel Maher wrote, "searching for recognisable forms" – searching for the kind of meaning that the De Quincey Company was attempting to produce in the Todd-Mparntwe Riverbed. And within this search for meaning, there was a search for the particular kind of meaning that the De Quincey Company was trying to convey with its use of the plant spinifex. In this sense, as something recognizable "was not forthcoming", the general confusion over the reception of *Dictionary of Atmospheres* was compounded by a confusion over what the Company was trying to convey in this very culturally and ecologically sensitive place, using this very sensitive cultural and ecological material.

Though audience members and reviewers did not comment specifically about the Company's use of spinifex, the final bonfire was significant – and emblematic of the joint problems involved with audience participation and the critique of insensitivity – on the grounds that the audience did not respond to the bonfire as the Company had anticipated. The Company was, in fact, very concerned with the nature of audience participation and the reception of images in *Dictionary of Atmospheres* and carved out a set of tactical approaches to engage audiences in a very specific way. Company members conducted trial runs with students at the University of Sydney and continually reflected upon and assessed the means by which they could communicate what was essentially a private language related to the Central Desert landscape to a public audience that had not shared the Company's years-long history of investigation of the area.

While *Dictionary of Atmospheres* was not meant to be a straight-forward narrative account of the years of Triple Alice investigation, director Tess de Quincey was interested in communicating at least a few of the qualitative values that participants had sensed and articulated amongst themselves regarding the effects of the desert on a human visitor. One of these values had to do with notions of gathering – of the desert space providing the means by which people could come together, to commune in the sands, to pause and sit around a bonfire, to share knowledge and energy across difference. The bonfire was meant to facilitate that gathering action, to provide the space and framework for that connection to occur. The Company's elaborate, labor-intensive process of gathering the spinifex, the quiet poetry of the women's dance with the spinifex bundles and the final burning was conducted not for merely aesthetic purposes. The bonfire was intended to provide that meeting place, that gathering place, that literal and metaphoric "burning point" (Gallasch with de Quincey 2000: 9; de Quincey in Finnane 1998; de Quincey 2003), which would serve as the final punctuation through which performers and audience members could commune. And it didn't happen. Not in the way the Company intended. Their intentions were betrayed by the brevity of the flames, by the confusion of the audience. And so the Company's invented spinifex ritual invoked a "poetics of failure" to the extent that it produced a state of "psychic and existential uncertainty" that was made manifest through the exploration of a particular "structural vulnerability" (Bailes 2010: xvii). The thoughtful rituals that the Company members had developed over their month of residency in Alice, derived from years of sensitive exploration of the desert space, undertaken to produce a particular outcome involving the *Dictionary* audiences stopping to pause and commune at the end of the performance, only led to the dispersal of audience.

The paradox is that not only did the Company's careful plan "fail", but that their tactics can be read as having a peculiar or even perverse quality. The Company wanted to gather people, to commune with audiences, and they elected to do so by utilizing a material and a practice whose history is deeply unresolved on a site-specific, regional and even national scale. Audiences searched for meaning, searched for a way to interpret the De Quincey logic, and were offered a set of puzzles or contradictions.

In the pages that follow, I wish to explore the utility of these conflicts and contradictions. To this end, with regard to such performances that take the chance of "getting things terribly wrong", I invoke Della Pollock, who explains that it is important to consider that "where there is error, there is possibility" (2007: 246). Pollock suggests that, in instances such as these, we might elect to substitute consideration of "the pleasures and power of improvisational error for anything like 'failure' to do things right" (2007: 247). In this manner, whereas "failure" might seem to be an efficacious way to frame this particular episode within the performance, to the extent that the performance exposed a gap between intention and reception, "failure" by definition nonetheless has the potential to eviscerate performance's potential by reinforcing a (false) sense of what is "right" or "correct". The notion of the gap between intention and reception as an "improvisational error" rather than a "failure" opens up a space of possibility for the power of such a gap, and in this sense invites us to consider the peculiarity of De Quincey's spinifex in performance as a "battleground where ideas and experiences collide, sometimes to produce new visions of life" (Probyn 2010: 89).

My discussion of failure in performance is informed by, but quite apart from Sara Jane Bailes' (2010) nuanced discussion of such. Bailes is interested in performances that intend to fail, that seek to fail, or otherwise purposely "stage failure". The value of staging failure is at the heart of my discussion. However, as De Quincey did not intend to stage failure, I am adopting Pollock's idea of the utility and power of "improvisational error" (informed by Russo's (1994) *The Female Grotesque*) to highlight the way in which the unanticipated results of the spinifex bonfire generated a set of narrative and political possibilities, because it challenged the "normative repetition of the same" (Pollock 2007: 246). This is an underlying theme in De Quincey's work – particularly their work in the Central Desert – also referred to as the "centre." Harrison (2000) explains that "so much work that 'goes into' and 'comes from' the centre is about representation – about land, about race, about what constitutes a voice or a presence within evolving notions of country" (8). Implicit within this observation is an understanding that the production of meaning in, around and about "the centre" can become trapped in normative modes and mechanisms of representation. While De Quincey's work operates from an awareness of the form and function of these projects of representation, Triple Alice and *Dictionary of Atmospheres* were designed to have more of an open-ended, experimental and improvisational relationship to the sharing of information and the constitution of knowledge. Linking

Dictionary of Atmospheres to its origins in the questions raised in the Triple Alice art-labs, Harrison explains:

> The aim ... was to imagine an experimental event which would act as a 'think tank', a database and a rich and ongoing informatic process. What is an aesthetics, or more accurately a poetics, which responds to locale in Australia? What's a useful and productive notion of exchange and collaboration in the context of information technologies? What is 'thinking' and 'practice' at a moment when thought is ... conductive and associative and when the "writing of space" is the primary and yet necessarily inconclusive medium for expression? (2000: 8)

To this end, De Quincey's work in the Central Desert has sought to "generate new ways of thinking about how we are related to history and how we wish to live in the present" (Probyn 2010: 89).

Tess de Quincey is emphatic that her work in the desert is a part of an "investigation of place", in which she asks questions about how places "enter and inhabit people and determine their language and being" (Grant with de Quincey 2006: 253). This investigation and the kind of performative language that it produces, which de Quincey understands to be inherently personal, she nonetheless believes is translatable to the general public. In fact, de Quincey and her Company collaborators created *Dictionary of Atmospheres* because they believed that the staging of this translation – the public articulation of an otherwise private language generated in Triple Alice – would be useful for audience members. And it is the very sincerity of the project, in its dedication to "engender[ing] experience and relation" to desert places that made the presentation of the paradox – and all of the site-specific truths and problems it references – possible (Grant with de Quincey 2006: 253).

The "problem moments" in *Dictionary of Atmospheres* are resonant with geographer Nigel Clark's discussion of Australian art as negotiating sensibilities that have been "uplifted from the metropolitan centres" and "unleashed at the colonial periphery" (2003: 166). Clark suggests that site-based artwork of Australia and New Zealand is often imbued with the presence of what he calls the "feral", a wild quality that surfaces in practices examining what it means to live a contemporary existence in these post-colonial landscapes. Clark writes that the animals and plants brought intentionally and accidentally – those elements that would come to run wild, run amok and even thrive in these countries as part of the colonial project – have left indelible traces in the experience of these places today. The "feral" in Australian art and performance can thus refer to the presence of feral things in content; it can also refer to practices and sensibilities that have bubbled up in response to problems associated with those feral things. In the case of *Dictionary of Atmospheres*, traces of the feral exist in material and practical forms. The feral also exists as an inadvertent aesthetic presence. "Feral" is a way of characterizing the resistance and disruption that occurred in the problem-moments of this production and is thus partially responsible for the disconnect between the artistic group's intentions and the audience's reception.

While Clark is interested in art works that take on images and sentiments regarding ideas of "displacement" and the "feral" in rather literal ways, in the case of *Dictionary of Atmospheres*, I would like to suggest that qualities of "displacement" and of the "feral" emerge in more subtle and unanticipated ways. The De Quincey Company dug up spinifex at a remote location, brought it back to the *Dictionary of Atmospheres* performance site, sculpted the material and set fire to it in performance. But they did not engage in these practices because they wanted to make a piece about "displacement" or the "feral." Rather, they wanted to create the circumstances, the environment, in which and through which audience members could connect and commune through celebration of the local landscape. And it did not work as planned.

In this sense, "displacement" emerges inadvertently in this performance practice. While the group is earnest in its intentions with regard to using the performance as a means by which audiences might come together and connect in a particular way, it did not intend to *show* or *demonstrate* displacement. Displacement emerged in spite of the group's effort to establish a common presence in-place. And it is the "feral" that produces or highlights this displacement: a feral or wild quality at work in the performance that is productive of the ruptures and disjunctures between the artists' intentions and the audiences' reception.

It is this feral or wild quality that made the "problem moment" possible. In the case of the spinifex, though the De Quincey Company engaged in a series of careful practices to contain and manage the plant and subsequently utilize its perceived power and essence to bring people together in a particular way, the plant, itself, defied them – it did not perform as anticipated and this disjuncture is partly due to the Company's limitations about how the plant actually exists in the environment and behaves in response to fire. This is the feral at work – that wild, continually resistant quality that is certainly not exclusive to the Australian landscape, but takes on amplified significance in this particular post-colonial landscape which is still processing a set of questions about belonging.

Keeping in mind Clark's remarks regarding the legacy of the colonial project in Australian landscapes and creative practices, I have appreciated the irreconcilable differences that have been produced in this "problem moment" in the De Quincey Company's site-specific performance experience described above. This moment inadvertently produced sensations and experiences of *dis*placement – knowledge about displacement – made manifest through, as Clark states, "objects, practices, and techniques" (2003: 166) that have been imported to the location and left to run wild, unaccounted for. In some cases, these objects, practices and techniques have thrived in their wild state, as have done the feral camels that populate the Central Desert landscape.[3] These histories of importation – of things, of ideas, of ways of being – have been explored in Australian literature, art, film and scholarship. And yet they remain unresolved. There is still substantial ambivalence about how to move and be, about the ethics of moving and being in Australian landscapes. It was only 2008, for instance, that the Rudd administration finally made the public apology to the Aboriginal stolen generations that so many Australians have wanted for years.[4]

Ambivalence about the histories of "settlement" in Australia lives very much on the surface of Australian cultural practices. Feelings and expressions of ambivalence resonate in projects like *Dictionary of Atmospheres,* and yet this particular the project was not designed as a means by which to address this ambivalence head-on. Rather, the project was about something else – a response to a desire to bring people together, to establish "the communal". And yet, by virtue of the group's attempt to establish "the communal", these other unresolved issues were able to emerge – the ongoing feel-

---

[3] Camels were brought to Australia in the 19th century to serve as the primary means of transportation for crossing the desert. They were abandoned once roads and automobiles took over in the early 20th century. The population is estimated at one million, which doubles every 8-10 years (see Edwards et al 2008).

[4] Sorry Day, the National Public Apology, was held on February 13, 2008, and was one of the first orders of business when Kevin Rudd became Prime Minister. Sorry Day offered a public apology on behalf of the Australian government to the generations of Aboriginal and Torres Strait Islander children stolen from their families by government organizations for decades over the course of the 20th Century.

ings and experiences of displacement, brought forward by the nature in and of the group's *practices*.

This is why the "problem" moment described above is of great use in understanding the value of *Dictionary of Atmospheres* and its relationship to larger questions about Australian feelings of ambivalence towards the histories of settlement that have occurred on the continent. Within the problem incident, ideas, bodies, documents, biota were uplifted from particular centers and unleashed at new peripheries. These intra-group activities were not meant to replicate or reenact some sense of the "original" displacement to which Clark refers. The group did not intend to make a reference to settlement, per se, nor did they intend to wrestle with or negotiate settlement as an overt theme. However, the logic driving the decisions to use the spinifex is reflective of an inherited logic about what a designated space and a particular place can provide in terms of resolution. The group's act of reorganization and re-placement was repeated, occurring again and again for many years within the Triple Alice context and, subsequently, the Company's performance practices in *Dictionary of Atmospheres*. Using the Central Desert locations of Hamilton Downs and Alice Springs as designated sites of practice, de Quincey set up periods of residency in which bodies, performance technologies, and everyday objects were imported from distant locations and organized, *placed*, within each site – constituting, on each occasion, a new, temporary "whole" from a set of fragments. This constitution of a perceived whole from various parts, enabled by the conceptual formulation of site-as-container, manifests as a meta-performative trace through de Quincey's various desert residencies.

These experiments have been conducted, in some respects, as if they have the potential to operate within what Merleau-Ponty would describe as the "pre-objective realm" of embodiment (2006 [1945]: 14), to the extent that Tess, the De Quincey Company, and participants in the Triple Alice laboratories understood their creative methodologies as having an ability to get below the surface of that which is merely representational, drawing them into intimate, sensuous, immersive encounters with atmospheres and artifacts of a given environment. At the same time, these cohorts of participants, among them accomplished scholars, artists and students, are keenly aware of the extent to which global space is, as Doreen Massey points out, characterized by "relations, fractures, discontinuities, practices of engagement" which constitute "cartographies of power" (2005: 85). Although there is a phenomenological bent to the practice, they are not operating solely from a reductive or essentialized understanding of the body. There is a simultaneous acknowledgement of the potential of such performance practices to uncover, to reveal novel information – or uncover novel aspects of otherwise familiar information – alongside a built-in self-reflexive critique of the limitations of those very processes of revelation. Accordingly, the possibilities and limitations associated with the idea of "habitus" are incarnated, to the extent that the groups involved articulate the experience as having "infinite capacity for generating products – thoughts, perceptions, expressions and actions" while at the same time understanding that the work's "limits are set by the historically and socially situated conditions of its productions" and so the "conditioned and conditional freedom" that the work provides "is as remote from creation of unpredictable novelty as it is from simple mechanical reproduction of the original conditioning" (Bourdieu 1990 [1980]: 55). Participants' perception of the "novel" or unique information that can be derived from these performance practices is held in constant tension with their own self-awareness of the historically, socially and geographically situated nature of their modes of production, and of the increasingly complex, interdependent, fractured and discontinuous nature of global relations and practices of engagement. This particular tension is significant because it is emblematic of and tied up in larger narratives of displacement at work far beyond the boundaries of the performance environment.

That audience members, critics, outside artists and academics would be troubled by the uncomfortable moments in *Dictionary of Atmospheres* is emblematic of the extent to which the De Quincey desert projects are tackling aspects of the ongoing public discomfort with the histories of settlement. Aspects of the performance backfired, producing experiences of displacement in spite of Company efforts to establish inclusion or a comfortable sense of placement. While Clark accounts for these intra-performative irruptions in terms of the "feral", Joanne Tompkins (2007) refers to these qualities in performance as aspects of "unsettlement": those aspects of the histories of British "settlement" of the land that refuse to be settled, that perhaps cannot be settled, but that are addressed directly and indirectly, intentionally and inadvertently in contemporary Australian performance.

Rather than reflecting on these problem moments as ruptures, as accidents, as *mistakes* per se, this study approaches these problem moments as opportunities for investigation. The durability of the differences – between what the artistic team had envisioned and how that vision was executed and received – and the irreconcilability of the problems as they have been staged in this site-specific performance, are indicative not simply of cultural and ecological insensitivity. They are indicative of a worthwhile, necessary, and artistically and conceptually valuable messiness that exists in the development and staging of site-specific performance in Australia.

These moments of perceived insensitivity, of perceived tokenism in *Dictionary of Atmospheres* could easily be dismissed as failed attempts at interculturalism. This study, however, re-reads the problem moments as useful paradoxes worthy of analysis. A simple categorical reading of these moments as "failures" – the reading assigned so far by audiences, critics and academics – eschews an opportunity to investigate the modes of production that led to the performance, and the extent to which these modes of production are intertwined with ideological assumptions about the function of art-making and the possibilities that exist in site-specific and place-based performances.

Furthermore, the group is emphatic that its work is about site, about place – *not* about interculturalism. This is not to suggest that just because a group does not identify as having an intercultural agenda, that it is therefore exempt from critique when it in fact does carry out intercultural work. It is rather to offer that, while there is value in critical response to aspects of the work as intercultural, there is another possible critical response to these desert projects that takes the group to task on its own terms: the terms of "place-based" and "site-specific". The team of collaborators involved in the making of *Dictionary of Atmospheres* were primarily concerned with matters of "place", understanding their engagement with particular landscapes in terms of establishing a metaphoric or collective relationship to a particular site. The actual engagement of each team was intercultural. And yet the team was concerned with identifying that it was not trying to carry out a cross- or inter-cultural work but rather work that was in concert with and about "environment".

This was not simply a matter of shying away from obviously difficult terrain. I hypothesize that the avoidance of a more robust discussion regarding the intercultural aspects of the De Quincey's desert projects has been due, in, in part, to a need to maintain control over the group's professional identity. Tess de Quincey engages in substantial work with the public and has had to walk a fine line, over the years of trying to gather support in the way of Commonwealth arts funding, about the nature of the work that she does with the public. The organization of government funding is such that professional groups are forced to identify as either doing "Community Cultural Development" (CCD) or professional artistic work. Tess does not want to be labeled as doing CCD. Tess has expressed that, in workshops and training sessions that she facilitated early in her career in Australia, participants often attended for reasons that she perceived to be outside the scope of her interests. By 2005, for instance, she felt the need to be explicit on public workshop publicity that her Butoh/BodyWeather training was not for therapeutic purposes. Accordingly, establishing the professional identity of the De Quincey Company as something apart from CCD is not about elitism, as much as it is about the joint pressures of establishing consistency in an environment of limited resources for artists, and about Tess not wanting to be responsible for aspects of public engagement that are not of interest to her. Establishing a professional identity that can meet the demands of public and private sponsorship is highly complex in the Australian arts landscape. Community Cultural Development refers to a range of practices and engagements between artists and community groups developing projects at varying levels of "professionalism". While any work of art – whether hanging in a museum or created with a group of school children – could conceivably fall under the heading of "Community Cultural Development", the criteria for CCD funding is designed so that interested artists must be emphatic about the *use*-value or the *service*-orientation of the project. This emphasis favors processes that can establish, through quantitative data, the material outcomes for community participants. While Tess understands all of her work to have use-value and a service-orientation on aesthetic terms, she does not want to be classified in a community-arts context as these are reputed to be the "other" (read: non-professional) arts – those practices in which substantial time is spent organizing groups of people and accounting for the outcomes of engagement rather than in working with a highly-trained group of artists. As an extension of this line of thinking, while there are intercultural aspects to many of her projects, she is careful to articulate that she does not *do* interculturalism or work *about* interculturalism, because she would then be held accountable on these terms. Her work is, most certainly, intercultural, and she has endeavored, in her desert projects in particular, to generate intercultural dialogue. However, the distinction here is one of practice rather than identification. Rhetorically, Tess does not identify her work as intercultural. Practically, her work is intercultural in many respects.

With *Dictionary of Atmospheres*, dialogue about interculturalism lived beneath the surface of the work. On the one hand, aspects of the intercultural informed and saturated everything that was done in the riverbed, in the sense that members of the predominately white Company were keenly aware of the inseparability of colonial history from their contemporary presence in the space. And yet focus within the performance-making environment was centered primarily on questions of place or location, conceptualized topographically. For De Quincey, a tactical logic with regard to the performance site gave rise to a microscopic analytical approach to place – cultivating performers' relationships to the feel of the sand, the experience of a hill, the spatial dynamics of a tree – as choreography which had been generated in Triple Alice and subsequently developed amongst Company members in Sydney was then positioned at different points along the riverbed.

The choreography was both "placed" in the site, as well as articulated into the site anew. In this sense, the objective was not simply to import precisely what had been crafted in a Sydney studio and re-create it verbatim in the riverbed. Rather, the choreographic material brought to the site was continually re-worked so that it could "meet" and converse with the logistical and affective dimensions of this new place. The choreography was thus made-again, as it was woven into the Company's experience of the Todd-Mparntwe riverbed – including their experience of being outsiders, city-siders, and (for the most part) representatives of "white culture". This layering of environmental information, imbued with cultural and historical information, is part of the BodyWeather training and performance-making technique. As Frank van de Ven explains,

> Body Weather is a comprehensive training and performance practice that investigates the intersections of bodies and their environments. Bodies are not conceived as fixed and separate entities but are – just like the weather – constantly changing through an infinite and complex system of processes occurring in- and outside of these bodies. (van de Ven 2013)

Van de Ven's description of BodyWeather as a practice that works at the interstices of bodies and environments, both of which are "constantly changing", sheds light on the process whereby De Quincey sewed material, ideas, perceptions and expressions collected in Triple Alice into the riverbed performance space in Alice Springs. Karen Vedel, dramaturg for *Dictionary of Atmospheres*, relates Tess de Quincey's perspective on the function of various sites in the development of the work:

> each site and each encounter presented a different 'contract', which was defined by the matrix formed by the geography, textures, speed, the intent and reality of the architecture, the history,

> the inhabitants and their expectations. ... while each site posed unique challenges to the artists through the sum of the particular components, their response to the assemblage relied on a repertory of corporeal techniques, which had been developed through their practice in Bodyweather. (Vedel 2007: 8)

Vedel's emphasis on BodyWeather as helping performers amass a "repertory of corporeal techniques" helps to clarify that the training paradigm is centrally focused to the cultivation of "physical presence" for performers (van de Ven 2013). Indeed, BodyWeather trains for receptivity in rehearsal and performance. While Vedel points out that De Quincey's "mapping" of a performance site "extends itself far beyond the physical features of the actual place to include also institutional, historical, ideological, social and cosmological characteristics" (2007: 8), social, cultural, historical and geo-political factors are considered "always already" at work – and so, here again, aspects of the intercultural are not overtly explored, but rather considered to be a kind of tacit information that exerts an influence and shapes the experience of the performing body.

The way that particular kinds of information – or, knowledge – are brought into the body in BodyWeather and categorized, conceptualized and translated into performance is complicated by the technique's operational notion of the "empty body" as a "starting point for movement" (Taylor 2010: 72). Australian BodyWeather practitioner Gretel Taylor critiques the role and presumption of "emptiness" in the technique, particularly when it is utilized in post-colonial landscapes:

> Until very recently, the overwhelming response by white Australia to these pervasive historical links has been denial. Whilst to white people white bodies are so normal as to be seen as almost lacking ethnicity, to Aboriginal Australians the presence of white bodies is a very visible constant reminder that, as Indigenous scholar and activist Aileen Moreton-Robinson (2003, p. 67) notes, 'our lands were invaded and stolen, our ancestors massacred and enslaved, our children taken away and our rights denied, and these acts of terror forged white identity in this country'. White corporeality, Moreton-Robinson continues, 'is thus one of the myriad ways in which relations between the colonizing past and present are omnipresent'. (2010: 82)

In Taylor's observation, we see a second tension at work in the De Quincey Company's production of *Dictionary of Atmospheres*. While Vedel points out that the "sum of the particular components" of each site, including "institutional, historical, ideological, social and cosmological characteristics" are included in the Company's engagement with and response to the riverbed, the BodyWeather technique, itself, stages within performers a kind of impossibility, to the extent that it asks them to use "emptiness" in the process of "dancing a place" (Taylor 2010: 72). As Taylor points out, the bodies of white performers in Australia are not empty, and they are not read or interpreted as empty. Thus, the staging of white corporeality in *Dictionary of Atmospheres* is yet another example of the way that the "details of the contract posed by this particular site ... remained excessive to any attempt to contain it in a matrix" (Vedel 2007: 13).

Despite the complications of identifying – or, not identifying – *Dictionary of Atmospheres* within the rhetorical framework or matrix of interculturalism, the De Quincey Company did acknowledge a intercultural issue that they felt was present in the specific site in which they were working: white avoidance of confrontational Aboriginal spaces, such as the Todd-Mparntwe riverbed. Karen Vedel describes the Company's observation of the space and the way it was used differently by different populations:

> Observations of the daily activities in the riverbed showed two very distinct spatial practices, which mirrored the *de facto* segregation of the population of Alice Springs. ... The only 'whitefellas' with a spatial practice that did not merely traverse the riverbed were either members of the local police, who regularly enforced their power of jurisdiction patrolling the riverbed in a motorized van. Or they were members of the local cricket team, who jogged in the sand as part of their weekly exercise. The persons, whose daily practices *did* engage with the riverbed of Lhere Mparntwe, were of Aboriginal descent. Moving either *alongside* or *in* it by foot, many chose the sands and the trails on the banks over the paved roads as their preferred route when moving to and from the Aboriginal communities on the outskirts of Alice. Furthermore groups, or 'mobs', of adult and elderly persons from the Aboriginal community, mostly males, settled in the shade of the red river gum trees in the riverbed. Forming circles in the sand of anything from three to around twenty persons, these groups fluctuated in size during the run of a day with persons drifting to and fro. Perceived from the outside, the groups' main activity was

> talking, often in quite full voices. And although drinking alcohol in public is forbidden, drinking *did* take place, especially in the vicinity of the bottle shop. The social challenges facing the community in the riverbed, which include violence related to substance abuse, was perceived as a threat to the upholding of both 'whitefella' and Aboriginal law. (2007: 3-4)

Through the myriad practices that the Company established while in residence in the riverbed – ranging from the daily removal of trash from the sands, to the gathering in circle formation to discuss the day's work, to the drinking of tea, and the exploration of the space in individual and small-group exercises – the De Quincey Co "added new spatial practices to those already existing in the riverbed" (Vedel 2007: 11). In this sense, they did not endeavor to stage an intervention, or to engage in overt intercultural dialogue with, for instance, the groups of Aboriginal men gathered in the riverbed. However, a subtle, nuanced set of exchanges did transpire over the course of the residency, which included casual conversations, the exchange of greetings, and even one shared performance experience. Vedel describes the composition of the audience for the performances od *Dictionary of Atmospheres*, and one poetic moment in which an Aboriginal man from one of the groups in the riverbed joined the dancers in their choreography:

> The four performances of *Dictionary of Atmospheres,* which were given free of charge, drew a substantial audience that was largely comprised of resident 'whitefellas' and tourists. As for the Aboriginal persons in the riverbed, who were well acquainted with the performance by the time of the premiere, the tendency was to either withdraw to the riverbanks or to remain in the periphery of what for a little more than an hour became a performance site. On one occasion, however, a group of Aboriginal men remained seated in a spot in the riverbed that was on the performers' itinerary. Not until the dancers reached them and proceeded to dance next to them, did they get up. While the group retrieved to the bank of the river, one man remained, entering into a movement dialogue with performers, and as they moved on, he took a bow before the audience. (2007: 12-13)

By staging the performances in the riverbed, the Company was not only staging their white corporeality, but also staging their desire to participate in the space, and to create temporary relationships with the site and its occupants. The group's approach to the cultural problem that they perceived – white avoidance of confrontational Aboriginal spaces – involved a circuitous route around the overt problem of interculturalism that permeates the history and contemporary experience of the riverbed. So it is a round-about kind of process. And yet, as the problem moments illustrate, whether via nature or via culture, the unsettled aspects of the histories of place that have produced the anxieties that the group wishes to confront are bound to surface one way or another. The exciting thing about the emergence of these problem moments is that they speak to ways in which contemporary site-specific performances in Australia are produced and also to how this particular site-specific performance revealed important negotiations in the politics of place that are often concealed in other public efforts at asserting a "sense of place".

Part of the problem of place and a "sense of place" is the very multiplicity that the term "place" and the phrase "sense of place" mask in singular form. At the start of his edited collection entitled *Making Sense of Place*, sociologist Frank Vanclay writes that, while "'place' is generally conceived as being 'space' with imbued meaning ... [b]ecause place is personal, a particular location can contain a range of meanings" (2008: 3-4). The place-based practices of the De Quincey Company operate on a formula designed to address the problem of multiplicity within the notion of "place" and "sense of place". The group begins from the premise that a site or specific place can act as a container of sorts – a container in which ideas and issues might be presented for a limited time. From this premise, the De Quincey Company goes microscopic – into the minutia of each Company member's personal encounters with bits and pieces of that place, establishing, for instance, affinities with individual trees (i.e. "Peter's tree") and hills (i.e. "Victoria's hill") – even as it understands those microscopic explorations as being informed by historical, cultural, social and geo-political factors.

In this sense, the performance group is working from the strategic premise of site-as-container in order to deal with the massive and unresolved problems of Australian place, which Sydney-based Performance Studies scholar Gay McAuley articulates as being related to the question of "how to live responsibly in this place" (McAuley 2006: 22). If place is, as Vanclay writes, constituted out of a range of personal meanings, meanings which generate forms of "attachment" to place, then, as McAuley continues, in Australia, "attachment to place is necessarily problematic," as "settlement" in the country "involved large scale unsettlement of the Indigenous population" (2006:

22). These histories, McAuley argues, are productive of "the fraught nature of the relation to place that predominates in Australia" (2006: 22).

Site-as-container may be the strategic premise informing the group's work, and the means by which they begin to address the problems involved with attachment to place, but the subsequent tactical differences are more specifically related to each environment – Alice Springs and surrounds – and the reasons why the group has been drawn to each desert location that it encounters. Karen Vedel theorizes that the approach to site-specificity taken by Tess de Quincey might best be described using James Meyer's (2000) idea of a "functional site", as a "process and an operation occurring between sites" (Vedel 2007: 8). "Temporary, mobile and allegorical" in nature, a functional site operates at the interstices of ever-changing bodies and environments, which is philosophcially compatible with BodyWeather as a technique. As a practitioner that literally works between sites – not only between desert sites, but between desert and city, between Japan and Australia – Tess and her work is always "occurring between sites" and must be understood as such.

Strangely enough, even though anxieties about settlement live on the surface of the public imagination, even though the relation to place is understood to be "fraught," there is a joint public exhaustion with these histories and a desire to tell other more harmonious stories. What are we to make of the sweeping epic film *Australia*, which softened the story of settlement and enraged Australian cultural critic Germaine Greer (2008) for its facile omissions? *Dictionary of Atmospheres* was not designed to be a counter-narrative, nor was it designed to be a resistant reading. In some important respects, however, *Dictionary of Atmospheres* as an endeavor represents an attempt to perform an idealized version of "community" and "communing". The problem moments disrupted the intentions, stood in the way of an idealized audience reception and were ultimately brought about by the irruption of some aspect of the feral – that displaced thing that cannot be contained and that continues to assert its displacement until it is heard. And then, even after it is heard.

Chapter Two

Spectacular Failures: Site-Specific Festival Performance as a Problem-Idea

What you see in the LA Festival is not what I think is important.
— Peter Sellars (2002: 137)

Site-Specific Problems in Festival Performances

Mention that a "problem" occurred within the context of the staging of the Alice Desert Festival and you would not surprise anyone who has had experience any of the Festival's iterations, as a performer or as an audience member. The Alice Desert Festival is an arts festival. By design, arts festivals rely on a whole heap of do-it-yourself initiative and a spirit of collaboration and adaptation that is directly related to converting public spaces into performance venues. What's more, the Alice Desert Festival is a community-based *regional* festival, markedly limited by a set of budgetary and infrastructural parameters: all the more reliance on the do-it-yourself initiative.

The Alice Desert Festival had its start in 2001, and was developed out of the place-based interests of small groups of local residents. It runs for approximately 10 days on a yearly basis, and features a combination of work by professional and non-professional artists, locals and visitors. Operating on a budget in the hundreds of thousands, which is generated by local, state and Commonwealth competitive funding schemes, the festival is supervised by a volunteer executive committee or "board" and employs approximately 4-6 full-time artists, organizers and technicians for a modest stipend during the months immediately before and during the festival. It relies on the volunteer labor of hundreds of community members.

Regional community arts festivals in Australia serve a unique function in the cultural landscape of this relatively young Commonwealth nation (British arrive in 1788; nationhood in 1901), whose population (which just exceeded

23 million in April of 2013) is disproportionate to the size of its land-mass (7.7 million km squared, though much of that is considered to be uninhabitable) and whose citizens live and work, by overwhelming majority, in five cities on the east and west coasts of the continent (Sydney, Melbourne, Brisbane, Perth and Adelaide). These big cities have their big festivals, which run annually on budgets in the millions and which draw international attention, audiences, artistic participation and even direction. Scholars have only recently begun to investigate the smaller regional festivals,[1] in part because they are a relatively recent phenomenon. In fact, even the reputations of the premiere festivals have only recently established a foothold. The oldest – the Adelaide Festival – was still getting its start in the early 1980's and the Victorian state government went through a number of names and iterations for a festival in Melbourne in the mid- to late 1980's before it declared its project the Melbourne International Arts Festival in 1990. And this is perhaps the most important distinction to be drawn between the smaller, regional community arts festivals and the premiere arts festivals in the major Australian cities: who came up with the idea. The big festivals were devised initially by state governments as efforts to stimulate the economy through support for the arts and for tourism. State governments also understood that this investment would generate national and international attention to the practices and talents in these Australian cities, attention that, government argued, would help build local, regional and national identities. The Alice Desert Festival, as small regional endeavor, was devised and developed at the local level through grassroots community efforts to articulate a local "sense of place".

The smaller regional festivals have complex identities that are always partially derivative from the larger festivals. The now-dormant Mountain Festival in Tasmania, for instance, occurred intentionally in the years opposite the Ten Days on the Island Festival – Tasmania's premiere state-sponsored arts event devised by the Bacon government in the late 1990's and implemented in 2001. In fact, the first Mountain Festival activity was held within the inaugural Ten Days on the Island Festival. Neither the Alice Desert Festival nor the Mountain Festival understands itself, formally, as being an alternative to the big festivals. However, artists and audiences who participate in these smaller festivals understand that they are carving out a different

---

[1] The Rural Cultural Research Network, sponsored by the Australian Research Council, held its first colloquium, "Festival Places: Revitalizing Rural Australia" at the University of Sydney in 2007. The Australian Humanities Review devoted a special section of Issue 45 (2008) to publications emerging from the colloquium.

kind of place-based identity, and this perception of "difference" is, in part, made possible by the pre-existence of the larger festivals.

The smaller regional festivals are produced through networks of known community artists, teachers and rehearsal spaces: modes of production that are designed to generate a particular type of collective experience and group investment in the collective. Regional festival activities contribute to the generation of local identities for the purposes of civic pride and also for the purposes of placing these regional locations – and particular sensibilities *about* these locations – "on the map" in a country where the perception has been, historically, that all of the cultural activity takes place on the "strange urban fringe to an empty continent" (MacKenzie 1961: 239). In other words, because the vast majority of the population lives on the eastern and western seaboard, and because the bulk of national resources exist on that fringe and continue to be allocated toward that fringe, these smaller regional endeavors are designed to redress aspects of their histories of being ignored, marginalized, and sidelined because of the perception that they are devoid of any cultural or economic significance. Sociologist Frank Vanclay refers to these processes of shouting proudly from the margins as "place-making" (2008: 6). Festival participants in these regional community-arts contexts are "place-making" in order to establish a collective sense of place that will reinforce the relevance of their chosen home and, further, will communicate the value of rural and regional locations in Australia to a national audience that has been historically oriented toward the major metropolitan centers.

These local festival identities are networked into larger systems that are productive of Australian national identities. To understand the relationship between festival performances and Australian national identities, one must acknowledge the extent to which festival performances exist amidst other rites of significance, with sport and spectacle being reliable sources of identity generation and reinforcement.[2] The 2000 Sydney Olympic Games provide a particularly apt example of the crystallization of national identities as they occur through sport and spectacle or sport-as-spectacle. In his analysis of the Opening Ceremony at the 2000 Sydney Olympics, Sydney-based performance studies scholar Michael Cohen writes that "the centrality of Anglo Celtic culture" and the myths of evolution in the history of Australia as na-

---

[2] The Melbourne Cup and the Australian Football League (AFL) or "Footie" Final are perhaps the two most significant sporting events that enact a strong sport/spectacle presence on the national stage.

tion were sophisticatedly reinforced through the narrative device of a "dream construct" (2006: 76). Organizing the Opening Ceremony as if it were a white child's dream – a dream from which the child never wakes – the performance conveniently erases the need for a presentation of historical specificity with regard to the telling of the national tale. "Dreams allow for representations of multiple, incongruent narratives and forgive the presence of contradictory and discontinuous temporal shifts: dreams take place in the ever-present" (Cohen 2006: 76). Spectacle, in this case, was a potent tool for communicating the kind of place-based ethos upon which local and national identities rely. And while certainly not all Australian spectacle is soaked in the kind of erasure that Cohen describes, spectacle is consistently used as a tool to establish a common ground upon which diverse populations might stand together. There are a number of possible ways to evaluate this process – of *doing* community through spectacle – but it is fair to say that the way spectacle plays itself out in public performances in Australia is dependent not only on budget and infrastructure, but also on the place-specific demands for articulating a community presence or experience.

Festival organizers understand the use-value of spectacle and regularly harness the power of the spectacle to do a particular type of work vis-à-vis community. We must understand, however, that the relationship between festival, spectacle and community operates differently in Australia than it does anywhere else in the world. After all, "community", writes art historian Lucy Lippard, "is as elusive a concept as home" (1997: 23), and this is especially the case in Australia, with its history of unsettlement, which lives very much at the surface of consciousness, its vast unpopulated spaces, and the fragmentation that exists in the distribution of the population. The experience of Australian place as fragmented is particularly punctuated when living in the "void" of the non-metropolises. In these marginal locations, there is a "longing to belong" (Lippard 1997: 292) as the "incomplete self longs for fragments to be brought together" with a *place* (Lippard 1997: 25). Lippard is writing about the ways that people in all sorts of locations desire to cultivate and maintain a "sense of place" – a sense that often involves the perceived power of a place to bring people together *through* connection to the land.

Enter spectacle as a problem-solving device. Spectacle is surprisingly flexible. When put into practice in festival contexts, it can be adapted to accomplish a number of different kinds of tasks with regard to rectifying community tensions and anxieties about attachment to place. Spectacle can at once circumscribe space and establish place. Spectacle can effectively crystallize an immediate, collective feeling of place through a highly charged emotional encounter. Spectators are invited to conduct a high-stakes emotional and physical inventory of themselves and their surrounds that is very much in-place. In this way, spectacle can do the work of both memorializing and bringing together feelings and experiences of fragmentation, so much so that feelings of fragmentation can *become memorialized* as they are replaced by the emotional impact of the present feeling of connection to place and to the others nearby who are bearing synchronous witness.

And it can be (seemingly) *easy*, terribly easy. As anthropologist John J. MacAloon observes, spectacle gives the "metamessage" that "all you *have* to do is watch" (1984: 269). On the one hand, MacAloon is describing the way in which spectacle can organize and mobilize a sense of place by rendering spectators as passive. On the other hand, MacAloon is making reference to the potentially transcendent and transgressive aspects of the spectatorship of the spectacular in performance – a reference which operates in conversation with other aspects of festival performance and meta-performance, such as Joseph Roach's (1996: 5) idea of "surrogation" and Georges Bataille's (1989 [1973]: 54) "aspiration for destruction". Roach and Bataille describe the ways in which festival performance can accommodate and encourage transgressive behavior. While Roach and Bataille are particularly useful is discussing the role of sport in Australian culture, as I discuss later in this section, participants in small rural and regional festivals in Australia are more concerned with consolidation than transgression. Or, in a sense, perhaps consolidation in those spaces might be seen as a modest form of transgression – in the sense that the rural and regional locations are staging their presence, their autonomy, and their performative power, which defies their marginality.

With regard to festivals that are *not* in Australia, performance studies literature has explored aspects of festival performance as producing moments of transgression that ultimately serve to reinforce the status quo. During festivals, participants are permitted to temporarily take on new and challenging identities in performance – temporary transgressions that end with participants feeling satisfied to return to their previous station for having had the opportunity to get the transgressive act out of their system. However, small rural and regional festivals in Australia are not about transgression but rather consolidation. They are not about the escapism inherent in U.S. festivals like Burning Man, so much as they are responding to a desire to negotiate feelings of living in a kind of "bantustan", which writer Thulani Davis describes as an "artificial [homeland] built for us by others on barren land" (2002: 23).

Davis' concept of "bantustan" helps to articulate the qualities associated with Australian place as being partially defined by its history as a "settler" country. Late 19th Century British imperialism rendered Australian place in a very peculiar way. On the one hand, British imperialism in Australia "incorporate[d] new land in the expanding British economy by conquest," using the justification of "*terra nullius* or unoccupied land" (Trainor 1994: 179). This proclamation of British sovereignty was in keeping with the imperialist project going on in other parts of the world. In Australia, however, at least one difference involved the *establishment* of sovereignty – in the way of white occupation of territories beyond the southeast corner – which Australian historian Luke Trainor argues was carried out very slowly because, among other reasons, "the Aboriginal population was perhaps three or four times larger than the computations of earlier historians had suggested" (1994: 179). Further, the period of occupation in Australia represented a "new stage" in British imperialism, characterized by an organization of Australia among "all the British land throughout the Pacific" which existed alongside a state-specific approach to the "colonization" of the Aboriginal people (Trainor 1994: 179). Within a discussion of these aspects of British imperialism, alone, there are at least three major factors that resonate within the current negotiation in Australia over determining a "sense of place". Guilt and shame over the nature of the "conquest", the evocative and damning associations linked to the definition of the continent as *terra nullius*, and anxieties over sovereignty and geographic identity in the face of state-specific approaches to matters of "settlement" are all defining qualities of contemporary Australian senses of place. Amidst all of the classical legends of Australian identity – the bushman legend, the pioneer legend, the legend of Ned Kelly, the bravery of the Anzacs – there is an overwhelming feeling among whitefellas[3] in Australia of being, as Australian sociologist John Carroll (1982) describes, *intruders in the bush.* "To arrive in a new and alien land, to build houses and towns, to join them with roads, even to clear the land and start to farm it, all

---

[3] "Whitefella" is a colloquial term for non-Aboriginal person. I use the term selectively in this study when "white," "European" or "British" falls short. Originally a slang word created by Australia's indigenous population to refer to the colonizers, "whitefella" is often used when describing incidences of white discomfort with the landscape during "settlement" and when describing contemporary race relations (Greer 2004; Cowlishaw 1999; Cowlishaw 2004).

this – the physical inhabiting – is much easier than the psychological settling of the country" (Carroll 1982: vii). While "many do now feel a little at home in Australia" (1982: vii), the psychological settling that Carroll describes is still very much ongoing, and it is being facilitated – and unraveled – in part, through festival spectacle.

Ultimately, the history of "settlement" is productive of at least three different anxieties or tensions within the formation of Australian identities: Australian identities and practices as merely "derivative" of a British or (in more recent years) American "original"; Australian locations as exerting a marginal or fringe influence in global contexts; and Australian identities and practices as tainted with the troubled history of genocide and ecocide that accompanied the European invasion. As Australian historian Paul Carter writes, it is the phrase "Debatable Land'' which "reminds us that the process of settlement was not a laconic replacement of one culture by another, a mechanical imposition of superior technology, a simple, physical 'taming' of the land, but, on the contrary, a process of teaching the country to speak" (2010 [1987]: 136). Neither here nor there, neither ours nor theirs, "debatable land" suggests the extent to which Australians continue to ask, as Stuart Grant and Tess de Quincey do, "How do I stand in Australia?" (Grant with de Quincey 2006: 248).

Ultimately these questions about Australian place-based identities exist no matter where you go, but they are posed differently from region to region and from festival to festival. The major, multi-million dollar festivals in Melbourne, Sydney and Adelaide, for instance, are concerned with using spectacle to demonstrate their connection to larger international conversations and practices as players on the global stage – that is the kind of "sense of place" that they wish to generate, a sense of a place that is connected globally, a sense of place that asserts an Australian city as being "world class". The smaller regional festivals utilize spectacle to carry out a form of missionary work, presenting tentative small-group findings on the nature of place that is more on the scale of a medieval pageant – beautiful, fragile, homemade and (frequently) a little bizarre. The differences in scale are productive of the differences in the outcomes of each attempt at spectacle: the bigger festivals accomplish slicker, more awe-inspiring feats. However, in investigating the ways that festivals employ spectacle as a means by which to generate a place-specific community, it is most useful to examine the way that different festivals manage spectacular failures.

Place ... Spectacle ... Community!

Even the premiere Australian festivals that have *international* budgets and reputations have encountered upsets and uprisings that are characteristic of the festival as a form. Problems can be expected with any endeavor that involves large-scale public participation. However, the distinction with these premiere events lies in their ability to subdue and diffuse problems as they arise because they, as institutions, have the resources to do so and because they, as servants to the masters that fund them, are under enormous pressure to do so. The Melbourne International Arts Festival, for instance, has the wherewithal to monitor and control conflicts, oversights and problems; it also has the responsibility to do so as it serves a higher cause. The Melbourne International Arts Festival was conceived by the Victorian state government, is funded by the Victorian state government (among many other major sponsors, public and private) and thus serves the Victorian state government (and its partners in industry). Like a minister ordained to preside over the intersection of tourism and the creative economies, the Melbourne International Arts Festival (MIAF) is, in and of itself, not just an extension of but a *form* of governance.

The MIAF, as a festival and as a form of governance, knows that it needs a public to survive. It needs the public to show up to its paid events and it needs to feed and reward the public by offering free events and opportunities to participate so that the public continues to feel a degree of ownership of and investment in the whole enterprise year after year. But the MIAF needs to do all of this on its own terms: the terms of establishing Melbourne as a world-class city that contributes to global conversations and practices. Enter spectacle.

In 2007, the Melbourne International Arts Festival staged its own version of John Cage's happening-inspired *Musicircus* on Federation Square.[4] It was an ingenious choice to solve the joint problems of world-class branding and public investment, as it combined the international name-recognition of John Cage with an event that, by design, could accommodate all manner of participation from both professional and non-professional artists, but would require little in the way of organization between all of the artists. A concept that

---

[4] Federation Square is a major intersection in Melbourne's Central Business District and home to a cluster of art museums, major performance venues, local tram stops as well as the train depot for all of the regional lines.

Cage developed in 1967, and which saw at least two iterations in his lifetime, *Musicircus* was designed to be an hours-long event of simultaneous, random performing by anyone and everyone that showed up at a chosen venue. All that MIAF organizers had to do – they thought – was find a venue, establish "start" and "stop" times, and get people to come out and *do* whatever kind of performance that they *do*. Organizers booked spaces on Federation Square, set a date and time, and created what they thought was a rather casual posting on the MIAF website of an at-large call for any and all types of performance.

The response was tremendous. So many groups, professional and amateur, volunteered to participate that the organizers had to withdraw their invitation after a few weeks – they couldn't have *too* many people showing up. The event itself proved to be both chaotic and exhilarating. From dusk until dawn on October 26 and October 27, hundreds of performers – children's choirs, chamber orchestras, small *a capella* groups – worked simultaneously at sites within the BMW Edge, the 16 channel sound system in The Atrium, outside in the Ecology Garden and on the Federation Square screen. There was din. There was poetry. There was cacophony. There were arguments. All things totaled, one could extract any number of "problem" moments with regard to public participation in the context of the Melbourne International Arts Festival's rendering of *Musicircus*. But it was controlled and it was smooth, because the MIAF has the money, the bodies and the infrastructure to keep a lid on a boiling pot. Melbourne-based theatre scholar Meredith Rogers, one of the organizers, expressed a degree of guilt over having had to pull the call for participation from the Festival website (2008). To pull the call was somehow to admit that the MIAF production of *Musicircus* was not *exactly* what organizers claimed it was about. A little disorder and chaos: yes. But a little goes a long way and the MIAF did not want the event to get out of hand. They wanted it to be clean. They needed for it to stay slick: not *too* many children's choirs and amateur *a capella* groups, we need to have a *few really good, virtuosic* groups holding it all together.

The smaller regional festivals in Australia understand the value of spectacle, as well, especially if it is a ritual spectacle. In Wollongong's annual community arts celebration *Viva la Gong*, there is an elaborate fire ceremony. The Alice Desert Fesival hosts a parade. The Mountain Festival curates a sculpture trail that runs along the rivulet descending from Mt. Wellington into the Derwent River. But spectacle operates in these spaces differently, as they are much more vulnerable to the kind of mundane interruptions and intrusions that can compromise the spectacular in the spectacle. Ultimately, spectacles in these spaces are awkward even when they are "successful" because the smaller festivals lack the means by which to leap from the ordinary to the extraordinary in the classic "fireworks" sense. In fact, the ordinary stays more-or-less intact.

The success of spectacle as it is staged in the smaller regional festivals is dependent on a tacit agreement between the producers of the event and the spectator/participants about what everyone is looking at. Everyone agrees that "*we* made this (gesture towards or attempt at) spectacle" and "*we* are continuing to produce this spectacle as (kind of) spectacular by virtue of continuing to look, continuing to participate, because *we know* most of the people here". The gaps between the ordinary and the extraordinary go largely uncriticized because the tacit agreement was made on the premise that what is *actually* spectacular is not the material thing that people are looking at, but rather that everyone is present and agreeing to look and agreeing to agree for this moment.

But it is this tacit agreement and the premise upon which it is made that leaves criticism and analysis in another kind of awkward, immobilized place. Because we've gathered and agreed to agree that the spectacle *is* the agreement, there is little room to lodge a complaint or a concern. How can you judge a child's costume in a parade without appearing to be an elitist snob? The child *made* that costume – shouldn't that be enough? From year to year, participants and audience members might endeavor to address problems with regard to the sloppiness inherent in community participation, but it tends to be left at that. If these projects get any attention from the scholarly community, it tends to either address the extent to which festival problems can be attributed to outside interference or funding pressures or it renders a nice, sanitized, feel-good description of the event and its significance.

This lacuna in the scholarship is a particularly unfortunate circumstance, because we are left with two kinds of accounts: those that document these small festivals as victims, held hostage by unfair funding schemes, misunderstood for the inherently "good" (social) work that they do; and those that document the festivals with a sanitation that suggests that they are unworthy of "real", robust assessment and criticism because they are "off-limits" (it's *kids*, how can we criticize *kids*?) or inaccessible (it's *artistic, I* don't get it, but the *artist* does). The fact of the matter is that the problems and the controversies in these small festivals, that are not getting talked about and are not getting written about, are perhaps the most interesting and useful aspects of these festivals. Further, the problems and the controversies in these small festivals speak to aspects of the on-the-ground, material reality of place and place-making that exists in Australian festivals both grand and modest. The problems and the controversies in the small festivals are not discussed or written up because they are not seen as important – they are just accidents, just sloppiness, just unprofessionalism. No. The problems and their associated controversies represent a complex – and oftentimes somewhat perverse – manifestation of public engagement that is enacting a powerful rebuttal to the manipulation of Australian narratives of place-based identity that stands to render aspects of regional festival governance flaccid. And they are waiting to be heard.

Carving Out Place

The De Quincey Co. *Dictionary of Atmospheres* performance described in this study can be traced back to 1999: the point at which the group's place-based research began in earnest. Over the course of seven years' time, the group, in the pursuit of its objectives related to community interaction, carved out a place for itself in relation to the Australian Central Desert. This "place" was both literal and figurative. For the De Quincey Company, carving out a place involved establishing a physical location in the Central Desert that would serve as an art-laboratory and then, later, a location that would serve as a performance venue. Carving out place also involved establishing a complex hybrid artistic-academic identity and recognizable *raison d'etre* in the Australian arts funding landscape through ongoing work in the desert.

Over the period of 1999-2005, the group (which was constituted differently on each occasion) made repeated migrations to specific sites in the Australian Central Desert. For Tess de Quincey, this involved three art-laboratories called "Triple Alice" held at the Hamilton Downs historic camp[5] in 1999, 2000 and 2001, followed by the performance of *Dictionary of Atmospheres* in the Todd-Mparntwe riverbed in 2005. *Dictionary of Atmospheres*, as the culminating event that represented the accumulation of place-based knowledge in the group's long-term study, can be understood as a project that mobilized a site-specific approach to performance-making as a means by which to generate a particular type of community participation

---

[5] Hamilton Downs is approximately 60km outside of Alice Springs, in the bush, though there is much debate among Triple Alice participants about that distance, rooted in whether one is measuring walking distance or driving distance.

through the transformation of public space. In *Dictionary of Atmospheres*, the De Quincey Company, a collective of performance artists based in Sydney, developed a performance that intentionally brought audiences into the sands of the dry Todd-Mpartnwe riverbed that runs through the town of Alice Springs. The site (which was distant and entirely different from the Hamilton Downs site where the previous laboratory work had been conducted)[6] was chosen in part for its aesthetic appeal but, more significantly, because it is an identified "problem" site: the makeshift campsite for dozens of displaced people, all of whom are Aboriginal. During the three weeks of rehearsals on-site that preceded the performance, the section of the riverbed selected for *Dictionary of Atmospheres* was populated by groups of these itinerant residents as well as the paddy wagons of the Alice Springs Police Department, driving through to monitor, discipline or collect these residents. Because of this dynamic, and the well-documented problems with violence in the space, the dry Todd-Mparntwe riverbed remains largely ignored by the white population of Alice Springs. The riverbed is known to be littered with the broken glass of beer containers, empty boxes of wine, cigarette butts and other detritus; and, it is known to be violent. For the duration of the rehearsal period for *Dictionary of Atmospheres*, the De Quincey Company took up temporary residence in this space and, in its four nights of performances during the Alice Desert Festival, the Company brought festival audiences to experience this site, as it was mediated by the performance. Thus, *Dictionary of Atmospheres* was conceived from the outset in relationship to the objective of bringing audiences into a disused public space to, at least in part, deal with the problem perceived to be *housed within* that disused public space.

The team that created *Dictionary of Atmospheres* can be understood to have been circumscribing space in such a way that allows them to use a *place* (as circumscribed, contained space) as a problem-solving location, to solve a perceived "cultural" problem using a "natural" environment (a riverbed). Environmental historian and theatre-maker Paul Brown writes that it is not uncommon for the Arts – and especially the arts in an Australian Community Cultural Development (CCD) context, to "explicitly announce themselves as a way of making meaning out of life, reflecting wants and needs, solving problems, and provoking critical debate about important social issues" (2006:

---

[6] The selection of the Todd-Mpartnwe riverbed as the site for *Dictionary of Atmospheres* and the differences between this site and the Triple Alice laboratory site is significant and will be discussed in detail in chapter three.

220). "[T]heatrical events, festivals, exhibitions, workshops, rehearsals" themselves become the "spaces" wherein this problem-solving can occur (Brown 2006: 220). For the De Quincey Co, an individual "place" or site offered the possibility for containment of an issue that was perhaps too big to effectively talk about. The logic followed that if the performance was contained in a particular site (albeit an inherently unwieldy site), that the perceived problem could be managed using aesthetic devices in that site. What the group did not anticipate was the extent to which the site would make its own contributions to their conversation. As the group sought to point out (or point *at*) the identified cultural issue, some aspect of the feral embedded within the site – as place, location, environment – brought forward a number of other issues related and unrelated to the issues at the heart of the artists' intent. The feral, as an unexpected place-based intervention, disrupted the story the group was trying to tell, producing a situation in which a new, less appealing story was playing itself out. These moments of intervention, or disruption, are "problem moments" – moments of rupture or failure of the production tactics to meet the artists' stated objectives – and they happened to crystallize in the group's attempt to stage spectacle.

Place ... Spectacular Failure ... Community?

The problem moment in *Dictionary of Atmospheres* was rather subtle – something you would only likely have noticed if you had observed the weeks of rehearsal prior to the final performances in early September, 2005 and if you had been privy to the Company's conversations about their use of the material spinifex. The Company, which employs materials explorations as a means by which to generate choreography, had gathered considerable amounts of the plant spinifex for such generative purposes in the weeks prior to the performance. A rough, prickly plant that grows in the desert sands, the spinifex was collected from a location about an hour outside of the performance site on two separate occasions and then brought back to the Todd-Mpartnwe riverbed and subsequently sculpted and bound into bundles. The spinifex bundles were then integrated into the final scenes of *Dictionary of Atmospheres* in such a way that the performance would end with the spinifex being lit on fire: spectacle.

The choice to use spinifex as the material that would enable the Company to create spectacle was (strangely enough, given the labor-intensive process involved in extracting the spinifex) a matter of convenience. While spinifex as a material resonates with the look and feel of the Central Desert land-scape,[7] it is also a powerful signifier of the ongoing, unresolved tensions between "whitefellas" and "blackfellas" in Australia.[8] Spinifex *looks* like the ground cover in the Central Desert but it *says* "I am a plant that has been historically valued by Aboriginal people and historically undervalued by European settlers." Lit on fire, it says, "I am a plant that Aboriginal people used as part of their indigenous firing systems, systems of land management that the European occupiers did not understand or value, systems that the European explorers and settlers used to track Aboriginal movements as a means by which to *establish sovereignty"* (to reinvoke the words of historian Luke Trainor). Spinifex has a life and a mind of its own. Spinifex has stories to tell. So, when given the opportunity, spinifex will speak. And this is what it did in *Dictionary of Atmospheres*. But, for the Company, the spinifex bonfire really was not about spinifex, it was about a gesture towards replicating their perception of a communal ideal, as they remembered it existing in Hamilton Downs, here on the sands of the Todd-Mpartnwe riverbed with groups of festival attendees.

The problem moment in *Dictionary of Atmospheres*, which revolved around the spinifex, occurred because there was a disjuncture between what the Company anticipated might happen with the spinifex bonfire and what actually happened with the spinifex bonfire. The Company had hoped that the spinifex bonfire would be a focal point for the audience, a gathering spot where the audience would remain following the conclusion of the performance. The Company believed that the bonfire would be an effective tool to make this gathering, this communing happen because they, as a group, had experienced the spectacle, joy and beauty of bonfires – first during their periods of residency at Hamilton Downs, and then during the rehearsal periods for *Dictionary of Atmospheres.* They had experienced the power of bonfires to attract a group's attention, to maintain a group focus, and to generate feelings of connectedness to the space and to the group. And so the spectacle of the bonfire made sense – not only in an abstract way, but in a visceral, embodied way. They, as a group, were able to generate a sense of connection

---

[7] While 25% of the Australian continent is covered in spinifex, it comprises up to half of the ground cover in the Australian deserts and "approximately ninety-six per cent of the plant biomass in local areas" (Haynes 1998: xv).

[8] Here am using the colloquial terminology because I found these terms to be used commonly when speaking to people in Alice Springs about cultural difference. See Cowlishaw 1999 and Cowlishaw 2004.

to place in Hamilton Downs – a sense of really *being* in place – in part through the gathering effect of a bonfire and they were subsequently able, as a small group, to replicate this sense of connection in the practice bonfires that they lit during the rehearsals in the riverbed. The bonfire carried out work for them – work that they thought was important.

The Company's desire to translate the power of the bonfire in their small-group context to the Alice Desert Festival context by keeping the audience in the space post-performance was directly related to the nature of the Company's observation of the Todd-Mpartnwe riverbed as a disused, undervalued place in the town of Alice Springs. Temporarily reinventing the riverbed as a performance venue, the De Quincey Company had an awareness that the staging of *Dictionary of Atmospheres* would have a perceptible impact on the way that the public engaged with the space, even if only for the duration of the performance. Punctuating the experience with a bonfire at the end was part of a strategy to hold audience members in the riverbed longer. However, partly due to the fact that spinifex burns very quickly and partly because most audience members seemed anxious to leave the space, the spinifex bonfire did not serve the desired function of keeping the audience in the space post-performance.

The choices that led to this problem moment with the spinifex were arguably felt by the audience, because the audience's behavior was affected by the moment. Instead of remaining in the riverbed following the performance, gathering around the spinifex bonfire, perhaps even sitting in the sand for a while and talking to other audience members or members of the artistic team, as was the Company's desire, the audience made their way through the darkness of the riverbed and disappeared towards the margins of the space. However, as the artistic choices that were responsible for producing the problem moment were woven into a set of other choices that informed the performance as a whole, the distinctness of this particular problem moment in *Dictionary of Atmospheres* was muted. The problem moment is not something directly addressed in the reviews of the piece – only subtly alluded to – and yet the problem with the spinifex is revealing of the Company's intentions and the Company's strategies for dealing with the Todd-Mpartnwe riverbed. The problem with the spinifex is emblematic of a wrestling with the problems of "place" and the crisis over the role and responsibility of a visiting performance group into a politically charged performance space that is specific to the De Quincey creative process.

Audiencing *Dictionary of Atmospheres*

If you were living in Alice Springs in August of 2005, you would have been hard-pressed to avoid the Alice Desert Festival. In 2005, Alice had a population of approximately 26,500. The Central Business District is made up of a grid less than 1 square kilometer, and contains a combination of shops that cater to the needs of the residential population (Kmart, Coles), the interests of tourists (photo stores, souvenir shops, art galleries) and restaurants that are both expected (Mc Donald's, Kentucky Fried Chicken) and unexpected (a vegetarian laksa restaurant and tea house). In August of 2005, most every shop window featured publicity for the Alice Desert Festival and register countertops were loaded with festival programs and leaflets promoting specific events and activities occurring within the festival, including show cards for *Dictionary of Atmospheres*.

The 40 or so people that, on the evenings of September 4-7, walked or drove down to the spot where the Schwarz Crescent intersects with the Todd-Mparntwe riverbed, just a block beyond Alice Springs' Central Business District (CBD), came down because they were involved with the Alice Desert Festival, or because they had seen publicity in the shops, or they had read about *Dictionary of Atmospheres* in Kieran Finnane's article in the *Alice Springs News* (Finnane 2005) or perhaps they had even heard the project choreographer Tess de Quincey and installation artist Francesca da Rimini speaking on the Australian Broadcasting Channel.

The audience arrived at dusk with a variety of implements. Some who were more familiar with the demands of the riverbed – and perhaps even acquainted with the De Quincey Company's strategy for navigating the riverbed – dressed casually, wore insect repellant, and had little in the way of excess gear. Others brought bicycles, lawn chairs, blankets and even picnic baskets. A number of audience members hovered on the edge of the riverbed for the first twenty to thirty minutes of the piece precisely because they were waiting to determine whether they actually needed to walk into the riverbed in order to participate in the experience. The spaces that came to be used as the "stage" and the spaces that came to be used for "audiencing" evolved over the course of the piece by design. Audience members were asked to be quite flexible from the outset.

Perhaps the easiest indication for most audience members that they were expected, upon arrival for the performance, to travel down *into* the riverbed, was the accumulation of bodies and technology already there, just past where the Schwarz Crescent pavement ends. Several technicians held small pieces of lighting equipment already illuminated and other crew members were taking photographs and holding small video cameras. If there was still some hesitation on the part of audience members regarding where they should locate themselves in the space, I eventually came along to distribute programs and my footpaths – improvised jetties determined by the flow of audience into the space each evening – were subtly suggestive that we were establishing a critical mass near a gum tree at the eastern corner of the intersection of the riverbed and the Schwarz Crescent.

The program was stark and white-black text printed on A4 card stock paper folded lengthwise. Before opening the program, one could already derive a sense of the history that led to this piece. "*Triple Alice Artists:* **Dictionary of Atmospheres**", read the cover page – the whole title in italics, with the first half of the title eclipsed by the boldface emergence of the latter half of the title. Most people in attendance would not know that Triple Alice was the name that Tess de Quincey had given to the three years of "art-labs" that she had coordinated at Hamilton Downs. However, once they opened the program, audiences would be familiarized with a few of these details alongside a number of other details, presented in both concrete and abstract terms: the names of local people who contributed to the art-labs; a quote from author Kim Mahood (2000) about "keeping a place alive"; a list of metaphorical themes that emerged out of the art-labs, such as "the performer as dreamer" and "swarm intelligence"; and a page of biographical statements for the key artists involved in the evening's performance. [9]

If an audience member was keen to make connections between the program's information and the information that was accumulating in this riverbed, which was actively being worked into a performance environment, then the matter of "swarm intelligence" might resonate just by virtue of the sheer number of production crew members in the space. It was as if we, as a Sydney-based company, had "landed" in this Northern Territory site, descended as a somewhat alien population. On any given evening, there were at least two dozen of "us" who were directly involved in the production. And while we did not look remarkably different from the audience members – most of us wore casual clothing that looked generally like the apparel of the

---

[9] "Keeping the place alive," "Performer as dreamer" and "Swarm intelligence" are markers that Tess de Quincey developed over the years of work at Hamilton Downs to organize the performance-based research on place conducted through the Triple Alice art-labs.

audience – our task orientation (with the distribution of the programs and the holding of the lights and the taking of the photographs and so on) distinguished us in the environment.

Arguably, all two dozen of us involved with the production were performing in that space. But only five were the designated performers. And these five were not immediately apparent in the space. Peter, a librarian and dancer in his 50's and the eldest of the five, dressed in tracksuit bottoms and a long-sleeved button-down shirt, both pieces absolutely saturated with three weeks of riverbed dust, lay quite still against the gum tree that provided the first scene of the piece. What with all of the other orienteering necessary for the audience members, who were familiar with this riverbed as a location but not likely familiar with being in this riverbed as a destination, Peter often went unnoticed for the first five or ten minutes of the piece, after which he rose to his feet with a monologue that began with the words "Life! Abundant life..."

At approximately the time that Peter came to life, three dancers, who had been posted at some half a kilometer up the riverbed to the north, on the other side of the Schwarz Crescent (completely invisible at first, from the audience's vantage point, and subsequently really only miniatures in the audience's perception), began to travel as one interactive body towards the audience. They wore translucent plastic raincoats, the pastel colors gently riding the surface of the riverbed's horizon, barely perceptible for quite some time at that distance, in the slowly diminishing light.

Finally, the fifth dancer appeared. Atop the boulders at the crest of Spencer Hill – the most distinctive feature of the landscape when looking in the northerly direction of the oncoming trio – there was Victoria, who, at about 900 meters elevation, was only made distinct by the yellow knit cap she wore and the large piece of red cloth that she held aloft against the evening's winds. Her moment at the top of the hill included a set of virtuosic leaps between the large boulders, the flowing red fabric floating in the air just behind her. And then it was clear that she was traveling, running, streaming down the side of Spencer Hill to meet the rest of the group at Peter's gum tree.

Peter's gum tree was thus a mustering point. By the time all five of the dancers were rallied around the tree, the audience would have begun to notice that a saxophonist was accompanying the group, breathing wind and water and other sounds into the instrument that were incredibly organic, incredibly human, rarely classically saxophone. The sounds emerged from the saxophone and also from elsewhere. Only after some time was it clear that several children and one adult were carrying boom boxes that amplified prerecorded CD's of the same saxophonist playing similar sounds, but all in different sequences.

From the mustering point at the gum tree, *Dictionary of Atmospheres* would continue on for another forty minutes and another 500 meters south into the riverbed, setting up scenes that were paced and punctuated through the use of a variety of properties. Dancers executed a slow sequence in which they looked into handmade mirrors and spoke the line, "I live in an Aboriginal country". Just after, they discovered lengths of red ribbon hidden in the sand and took off running, one at a time, toward another gum tree to the southwest. As the audience lumbered along behind the agile dancers, who had learned how to travel lightly atop the riverbed's sands over their weeks of site-specific rehearsal prior to these performances, the night crept in quickly. As the shadows lengthened, the dancers found a length of caution tape, which was first brought out and manipulated among them and then subsequently used to entangle the audience in bunches and bundles in all sorts of curious ways. The audience was good-natured about all of it: the uncertainty of what would happen next, the abstraction of the choreography and text and music, the obvious, literal ploys to rope them in to the experience.

When the dancers abandoned the audience, who were tied up in the caution tape, they left a group of people who, for the most part, were smiling. They were tickled by the clownish antics of the dancers, even if they did not entirely understand the reasons behind the performers' choices. At this point in the performance, the shadows of the evening had crept in remarkably quickly. It was only by virtue of the dancers' rapid change in location – running away from the gum tree where they had tied up the audience and towards an area in the riverbed 100 meters southward that had been set with three 14' x 20' screens featuring more colorful abstract imagery – that one might recognize how much light had been lost.

The remainder of the choreography was carried out in this final circumscribed space, where the dancers continued to work through a variety of scenes, all of which were now framed by the glow of the three enormous projection screens. By the time the two and then three women had suited up in their translucent raincoats and were carrying bundles of spinifex across the riverbed, cutting an east-west path that bisected the overall north-south flow of the performers and audience down the riverbed, everyone was feeling a bit tired. When the spinifex was lit on fire and gave off its quick, bright red light and the dancers disappeared alongside a trail of tiki torches that continued the southerly flow down the riverbed, you could feel the audience take a breath on their own and then give themselves permission to let their participation end.

In the final estimation, the De Quincey Company most emphatically employed elements of production that were designed to engage their audiences interactively. The De Quincey Company, having identified the Todd-Mparntwe riverbed as a problem site, endeavored to work through this problem by bringing audiences into the space so that they would be engaged with the riverbed. It was an imperfect translation of intentions. And in many respects it was not really even a translation so much as it was a transposition – a re-placing or re-arranging of elements that had originated at the art-labs at Hamilton Downs, and then grown out and inflected by the rehearsals at the University of Sydney, which had little to do directly with the politics of place of the Todd-Mparntwe riverbed.

To this extent, the problem moment identified here is the last moment in which the De Quincey Company endeavored to cultivate audience participation. Though the audience would not have known it, the burning of the spinifex was designed as a means to create a "gathering point", an ending location where the performance could conclude and where the audience could *stay* in the riverbed. The audience would not have recognized the burning of the spinifex as an invitation to stay in the riverbed, post performance, because the spinifex bonfire finished so quickly. And, further, the dancers had run off. The lights that had followed the dancers through the riverbed were gone, as well. There was nothing to keep the audience in the space. The audience was brought into the space with a mysterious set of cues and clues as to why they were there and how they were to participate. In some respects, the spinifex bonfire, as the culminating event, was an implicit gesture for the audience to make a leap in their perception from the riverbed as hostile space to the riverbed as space for communal cohabitation. This is a demonstration of a dream out of context, a *Dictionary* in a foreign language.

The audience would not likely have identified the burning of the spinifex as the problem (though they may have found walking in the riverbed post-performance in the dark to be a problem). However, the problem moment here – the disjuncture between what the artists wished to happen and what actually happened – is useful because it illuminates a whole set of strategies that the De Quincey Company employed in order to deal with the cultural problem that they perceived to exist in this natural environment. The problem with the spinifex thus illuminates aspects of the way in which the whole of *Dictionary of Atmospheres* can be understood to be a "problem" in the sense that the project is actively engaging with the perplexing, difficult issues surrounding of the riverbed-as-place through the vehicle of performance-making. The spectacular failure of the spinifex bonfire in *Dictionary of Atmospheres* thus becomes an interrogation of these perplexities, a proposition of how to manage these difficulties.

The problem moments thus reveal themselves to be valuable analytical tools in terms of their potential to contribute to an understanding of contemporary site-specific performances that have marked place-based interests. The problem moment described is not simply a mistake that occurred in an otherwise air-tight performance. Rather, even though the problem moments stand out as observable "mistakes", they actually "fit" into the whole of the performance and, further, are "fitting" as they reveal aspects of the whole that other elements of the performance are better at concealing. In some respects, the other parts not only "keep a lid" on the problems of place-in-performance, the other scenes in the performance actually obfuscate significant truths about the constitution of these performances, the points of intentionality from which they are developed, and what they serve to do – and not do. In other words, the problem moments are revealing of the extent to which site-specific performances are "problem-ideas" (Kwon 2002: 4) – projects that endeavor to deal with a particular place-based problem through performance research.

For the De Quincey Company, the spinifex bonfire in *Dictionary of Atmospheres* was intended to operate as a gathering spot, a gesture of inclusion of a cross-section of community members who infrequently traversed this riverbed location. The bonfire was also devised to be a means by which to establish a connection between those who were visitors or outsiders to this place and those that live in Alice on the margins, on the fringe of the town. Audience members and performers did gather, but did not stay. Outsiders and insiders established a temporary presence, but not necessarily a connection. Arguably, it was not possible for this moment to effectively, seamlessly render such a connection. There were other moments in which a connection was more evident – moments during the rehearsals for *Dictionary of Atmospheres* in which members of the production crew shared stories and anecdotes with the people currently living in the riverbed. A few times, Company members danced together with the riverbed's residents – though even this kind of interaction was met with a certain degree of trepidation amongst the entire production crew. In some respects, the irony of this trepidation in light of the Company's desire to interact was not lost on group members, who understood that it was this very fear – and a collective inability to find words to articulate these feelings – that brought them into the riverbed in the first place.

The De Quincey Company initiated the creative process by identifying a "cultural" problem of significance within the local community: reflecting a particular kind of knowledge that they had acquired over the many years of place-based research carried out in relation to previous De Quincey creative processes. The team of artists subsequently endeavored to create a performance piece that would address this cultural problem within the boundaries of a specific natural environment. In this sense, the artists sought to *contain*, or *pin down*, a specific cultural problem within a circumscribed and yet, in some respects, unrelated natural environment. The attempt at containment via site-specificity thus backfired, as the specific site ultimately contributed a number of other issues and problems related to the nature in and of the performance space, itself. These place-based issues and problems intertwined with and further problematized the initial "cultural" problem selected by the performance group in the initial creative process. A series of problems hypo(below the surface), hyper- (above the surface), and meta- (between various surfaces), were consistently at play within the performance environment, illustrating the extent to which site-specific works do not, in fact, serve effectively to "contain" spaces. Rather, site-specific performances expose the extent to which *place* is not so much a location as it is a consistently developing actor or player in the dramas that transpire upon and within it. But what can be gleaned from the useful problems?

Problems of Culture Staged in Festival Contexts

Director and festival organizer Peter Sellars has remarked that "what you see in the LA Festival is not what I think is important" (2002: 137). Delivered in the context of a speech that he gave at an international conference with a theme of "Multiculturalism in the Arts and Society" in 1996, Sellars is making reference to his own growing understanding of the function of arts festivals – even major arts festivals – that he has accumulated over his years as artistic director of the LA Festival (Los Angeles, California). In his lecture, Sellars goes on to provide an anecdotal story of a controversy that took place within the mounting of the 1990 LA Festival that represents the beginning of a series of epiphanies that he had about the use-value of mistakes in a festival context. Sellars explains that he and a committee that "read a lot of poetry" (2002: 137) but were not familiar with Salvadorean politics, invited poet David Escobar Galindo to participate in the festival. It was not until Sellars "came to work one morning to find [his] office occupied by fifty angry artists", and his desk "taken over and the entire place…occupied by angry artists" from El Salvador (2002: 138) that he was brought to realize that Galindo was "the right-hand man" of "the leader responsible for the death squads" from which Los Angeles' substantial population of Salvadoreans were refugees. This conflict became an opportunity for Sellars and the LA Festival to educate themselves about Los Angeles and the people who live there. Subsequently, the 1990 Festival was significantly reorganized towards meaningful community participation – a change that has had an enduring impact on the LA Festival in perpetuity. Sellars sums up the lesson in the following way: "You have to be willing to make a big mistake because it leads somewhere. You'll meet people you needed to meet. Allow that to happen" (2002: 138).

Sellars is talking about a problem moment that occurred in the context of a major festival – on the scale of the Melbourne International Arts Festival. And, like the problem that occurred in the staging of *Musicircus*, while the controversy is useful and revealing, it is also contained and mediated in such a way that it was not brought to widespread public attention until and unless someone centrally involved in the controversy decided to give a lecture about it to a select, sympathetic crowd. The conflict and the controversy in the 1990 LA Festival were contained wihin Peter Sellars' office, as he describes it. And while it is a presumably noble gesture that Sellars and the Festival committee elected to use the controversy as an opportunity to make a change that they felt was necessary, there is an aspect of the drama, as Sellars describes it, that reeks of the complacency-inducing resolution that Brecht identified as problematic in bourgeois theatre, in which "the spectator" is "allowed to submit to an experience uncritically…by means of simple empathy with the characters in a play" (Brecht 1992 [1936]: 71). It is inspiring to hear Sellars' tale, but it is ultimately left neat and tidy because *he* handled it, *he* processed it.

Controversy is processed and pasteurized in a variety of innovative ways by major festivals. In Tasmania's premiere Ten Days on the Island Festival, a latecomer to Australia's national festival scene, a funding scandal irrupted on the public front that spawned a major protest among artists and environmentalists in 2003. Ten Days on the Island, as Tasmania's state-defining festival designed with the expressed purpose of attracting international attention to the island's arts and culture, suffered from an at-large protest and boycott among Tasmanian artists, performers and writers, due to a controversy over sponsorship by a company associated with the deforestation of the island. This was a major problem moment that generated a recognition among Tasmanians that festivals are public property. They take place in public spaces. They require public participation – in the way of attendance and often also in the way of purveyance. And, as is the case with Ten Days, arts festivals are often touted as doing work *on behalf of* a localized public. When the work carried out by the 2003 Ten Days, purportedly *on behalf of* Tasmanian artists, was sponsored by a company that those artists hold responsible for clear-felling significant portions of the island's forests – Gunns, Ltd. – the artists withdrew their participation. "Not in our name", read the protest signs at the rally held adjacent to the launch of the 2003 Ten Days on the Island International Arts Festival.

While subsequent Ten Days Festivals in 2005 and 2007 have suffered a bit from the bite of the reputation damage of the 2003 protest, the anger has largely dissipated as the Festival has remained competitive – offering, for instance, the largest literary cash prize in the nation. The festival has also gotten better at hiding the names and identities of its funders. Ten Days was also successful directing blame away from the 2003 festival by scapegoating artistic director Robyn Archer for colluding with Gunns. Archer was ultimately replaced as festival director by Elizabeth Walsh. In an interesting coincidence, Peter Sellars, himself, was "sacked" as the artistic director of the 2002 Adelaide Festival after he proposed an unappealing "programme built around ecological sustainability, truth and reconciliation and cultural diversity" (Brown 2006: 220). Sellars was the first non-Australian appointed by the Festival Board (Martin and Sauter 2007: 97). In addition to a series of highly controversial choices regarding aesthetics, sponsorship and advertising, Sellars "strove for a community-based, free events festival, celebrating Adelaide as an aboriginal landmark," whereas "Adelaide represented by sponsors, newspaper editors, board members and other influential people wanted their international, spectacle-guaranteed and box-office-oriented festival" (Martin and Sauter 2007: 107). After Sellars was terminated, his program was subsequently "diluted with more traditional fare…testimony to the challenging debates cultural activities can spawn" (Brown 2006: 220). The major festivals *rectify* their problems.

Peter Sellars' observations that "what you see is not what is most important" and "you have to be willing to make a big mistake" are nonetheless useful insofar as they redirect attention away from formalist aesthetic outcomes and box office outcomes and towards the value of measuring a festival's success based on a framework that understands an arts festival as a cultural process. Remarking on the 2004 Adelaide Festival's "huge" programmatic and financial success in comparison to the 2002 Festival, which was marked by Sellars' influence and termination, Jacqueline Martin and Willmar Sauter observe that perhaps "Sellars started the ball rolling in trying to bring the 'local' to the Adelaide Festival" – a theme which the subsequent director for the 2004 festival was able to adopt and modulate successfully (Martin and Sauter 2007: 118). Martin and Sauter note that, whatever the case, it is clear that "issues of power, finances and politics determine the success of a festival" (2007: 118).

Tripling of Public Engagement and the Accidental Sense of Place

Miwon Kwon understands site specificity in contemporary art practice – and especially "project-based art" operating in more "public realms" (2002: 3) that result in "art-as-public-spaces" (2002: 5) – as a "problem-idea, as a peculiar cipher of art and spatial politics" (2002: 2). Kwon's observation is more directly linked to projects on the scale of *Dictionary of Atmospheres*. Building on Sellars' argument that "what you see is not what is most important", and Kwon's notion of project-based public performance art as a "problem-idea", I would like to argue that the problem moments in these smaller, regional festivals are useful because audiences *get to see* the problem. And they get to see the problem because these smaller regional projects as places made them possible. In the larger festivals, you simply do not see the problems – you wouldn't be allowed to see them or, at least, not for long.

The reason why you get to see the problems in these smaller festivals is not simply because they lack the infrastructure to cover them up, or prevent them from happening in the first place. The reason why you get to see the problems goes back to the formula upon which spectacle in these low-budget endeavors operates. Spectacle in these spaces operates based on that tacit agreement between artist and spectator/participant that, though the spectacle lacks the awe-inspiring qualities of the large-scale spectaculars, that the spectacle *is* the momentary agreement to agree that exists between all who are present. This agreeing to agree, which constitutes the spectacle in these small regional festival environments, is constitutive of the same problem that has prevented conversation about the problems in these smaller festivals, the same problem that has limited the critical response to these smaller festivals. And it is generated out of what I refer to as a tripling of public engagement that is made possible by the three elements of public-ness at work between a public festival, that is hosting an event in a public space, which relies on the labor of a significant number of public participants. Public participants in these instances are not just contents, as they were for *Musicircus*. In fact, when the public perceives, in these small festival spaces, that someone or something is being used *as* mere contents, there is a pointed outrage.

Problems are able to emerge for public staging in these smaller regional projects because: 1) the modes of production and networks of activity upon which each festival relies, 2) the sites in which the performances occur and 3) each festival's self-made identification as a community-oriented festival create an environment in which artist/participants feel more directly responsible for what they see. And it is this tripling of public engagement that also makes the problem-moments possible, inadvertently highlighting the work that needs to be done in each community that, until the "mistake", the "accident", was too formidable, to huge a topic to even talk about. If these problems are not addressed, however – and they usually are not, as they are dismissed as indicative of the kind of inadequacy often expected with community arts projects – there is a danger that these festivals will pass out of existence, deemed unworthy of future funding because they cannot deliver the product that they were pressured by funding bodies and government agencies to deliver.[10] Without a critical voice speaking up for these problems, there is, further, a danger that the better-funded, infrastructurally-stabilized festivals already underway at the state and national levels – events which deny the kind of truly local, grassroots specificity in which these smaller festivals specialize – will go unchecked, and we will miss an opportunity to examine the tactical, on-the ground realities of the populations and stories that find a voice (albeit in an imperfect form) in these regional environments.

---

[10] This has already eventuated, in part. The Alice Desert Festival went underground after the 2005 iteration because it was deemed to be infrastructurally unsustainable and was placed on hold until 2009. After this period of dormancy, the Alice Desert Festival is now back up and running. Tasmania's Mountain Festival, discussed briefly in the early part of this chapter, had its last formal iteration in 2008, after which time the Festival Board fired the founding director.

It is in this way that these small regional festivals reconfigure our understanding of the elusive concept of *place* in an extraordinary way. Place has been a consistently contested term, a contested concept. Tracing our understanding of place back to the ancient Greek, we find three words that account for some understanding of place: *topos* (space/place), *chora* (space/place) and *oikos* (home). There is no single word for place. Rather place is always composed through a combination of things that can be understood not only as a combination, but existing as a tension between a number of elements in its composition. Place is literally, linguistically, conceptually and phenomenologically always being made, always under construction. Further, understandings of place are always interdependent on understandings of space and spatiality.

Existing approaches to the study of place and "sense of place" can generally be categorized into three groups: place as simple location; place as an assertion of special character or significant locale; and place as existential. The humanistic approach to the study of place is best characterized by the work of geographer Yi Fu Tuan (1971). For Tuan, place is space plus meaning, which is brought into space by humans, who derive this meaning from the core of felt values. Here, place is a psychological or experiential construct, where experience constructs reality. The second sense of place is reflective of the research of philosopher and phenomenologist Edward Casey, for whom place is a mere modification of space (1996). Casey is primarily concerned with articulating the distinction between space and place, identifying places as not locations but *happenings* (1996). In his article "The Memorability of Inhabited Space" (1991), Casey identifies memory as a crucial element of self, which is tied to place and location. In this trajectory, Casey establishes that there is a self, which, working backwards, is composed largely out of memory. Traveling further backwards on this trajectory, memory is placed or sited and thus the equation goes: self – memory – place. Or, places beget memory and memory begets self. Thus, self is defined and constituted in relation to place(s).

The third sense of place, which is articulated in the work of Jeff Malpas (1999), is written in reaction to the perception that the perspectives of Casey and Tuan reinscribe a nature/culture dualism in which culture, heritage and "sense of place" are always in addition to or separate from place, as such. Malpas understands place in an existential capacity, in which existence is essentially relational. In this way, place and existence are intertwined, where we are who and what we are in relation to place and the specificity of where and how we are located. Here, place is not only simple location, nor is place extant only because humans attach meaning, events, or memories to it. Rather, place is understood in terms of the greek *chora*, which stands to represent space/place with particular reference to "the receptacle" or "the womb". Place is that space within which things come into being.

When we then observe performances in these small "sense of place" festivals and the problems that (are allowed to) emerge within them, if *place* is approached as composed of a series of relational arrangements, then Malpas' model of place as "womb" may likely be most useful. The festivals are the sites, the locations, the places wherein the problems are allowed to happen – permitted to come into being. The "problems" in these small, regional endeavors help demonstrate how these festivals *as* places are able to illustrate, for public consideration, particular types of problems that the larger, slicker, better funded projects would never allow to happen – they simply could not accommodate an accident or oversight on this scale.

The ruptures in the spectacle that constitute the "problem" can be understood as the "feral" at work, which is allowed in through the tripling of public engagement. In the larger festivals, the feral is effectively tamed and caged because the resources exist to do so. The actual social and cultural function of the presentation of the problem in the small festival context is the bursting of a bubble of a myth that has been told about place and community in each location. The rupture and the controversy that ensues render flaccid the lie that the festival inadvertently presents by way of its attempt at spectacle. The rupture reveals that the festival, in some respect, is not what it says it is about. Strangely enough, this breakdown – though inadvertent, uncomfortable, and often unnoticed – actually generates the "collective" that each festival wanted, after all. The genius of the breakdown of the spectacle is that it draws people together through its own inadvertent failure – it allows people to experience a shared observation of truth about place that they generate themselves through unsolicited response to a perceived problem, as opposed to experiencing an imposed truth of a grand, "successful" spectacle.

We go to the big shows – the Olympic Opening Ceremony, the *Musicircus* event – but do we really believe the spectacle that we see there? Do we connect with it narratively? Does it really do the work of reinforcing a collective identity? The wonky, embarrassing problems of these smaller festivals, in a way, are perhaps a better means by which to identify what the public audiences in each case really care about because their offense, their anger, their confusion is palpable. These emotions do not necessarily generate the kind of collective, utopic sentiment that the De Quincey Company had envisioned, but the spectacular failure did connect audience members to their feelings about place, which is to say that it connected them to their "sense of place" and represented a form of "place-making".

The accident is perhaps the most tangible, the most potent thing happening in these performances; and it provides insight into aspects of DQCo.'s relationship to place. While Australian regional identities are being shaped in the context of the "carving out of place" that occurs within the rhetorical and staged *doing* of the Alice Desert Festival, *Dictionary of Atmospheres* as a "sense of place" experiment invited unanticipated observations and controversies about a particular site to "come into being", to come to the surface of consciousness. The next chapter will address in greater depth the series of art-laboratories, rehearsals and practices that led up to *Dictionary of Atmospheres*, as an attempt to further explore the embodied philosophical perspective of Tess de Quincey and her collaborators towards the desert environment. It is a microscopic approach to place that characterizes their process, which is, in part, founded on the premise that investigation of one place can lead to a relationship with another.

Chapter Three

De Quincey in Alice:
Transposing Place in the Central Desert

I thought Australia,
I thought,
yes,
Lake Mungo and then to the Centre!
I was dying to go to the Centre.
And of course,
10 years later I get to Alice for the first time.
And then comes the fascination:
What is this continent?

– Tess de Quincey ('RealTime')

The Alice Desert Festival, as a small, regional community-arts festival "place" – or, in Jeff Malpas' (1999) understanding of place, "womb" – made the presentation of *Dictionary of Atmospheres* possible by providing the space and infrastructure necessary for the De Quincey Company to share their work. The festival thus also made possible the presentation of the paradox of the De Quincey Company's engagement with the plant spinifex. But was the burning of the spinifex a problem associated with the making of "place" in a festival context? An issue bound up with the Company's process?

The work carried out by the De Quincey Company in the context of the Alice Desert Festival involved the intersection, collision and confluence of energetics imported and autochthonous, indigenous and invented, expected and surprise, visible and invisible. "Burning point" is the phrase that Tess de

Quincey[1] uses to describe the process of bringing her Japanese BodyWeather technical training to an investigation of Australian place (Grant with de Quincey 2006: 247; de Quincey 2003). "De Quincey describes Alice Springs and the Central Desert as a 'burning point, geographically, culturally and politically' and 'the confronting heartbeat of the continent'" (Finnane 1998). In analysis of *Dictionary of Atmospheres*, which represents (to date) the culminating activity in a particular strand of that research, there are a number of "burning points" at work. The problem with the spinifex can be understood as a bringing to a head, or a confrontation between an established set of processes that were highly individualized and substantially private (or, at least, cloistered within the setting of the Triple Alice art-laboratory environment) and the complexities of staging those processes for the first time in a very public and politically-charged site.

In order to fully appreciate the logic informing the De Quincey Co decision-making involved in the gathering, sculpting and burning of spinifex in *Dictionary of Atmospheres* and how that logic reacted to the logic of the Todd-Mpartnwe riverbed as a site, one must travel back to the Triple Alice art-laboratories that de Quincey carried out in Hamilton Downs 1999-2001. The art-labs are part of a larger body of de Quincey's work that began in Lake Mungo in 1991 and that continues to this day. Tess describes the intentions that shaped the Triple Alice art-labs in the following way:

> [These performances] weav(e) a field of research which pendulates between the city and the desert [...] comprised (of) both long and short as well as very fast and very slow processes. (de Quincey in Grant with de Quincey 2006: 253)

For de Quincey, who is based in Sydney, but does quite a bit of domestic and international traveling as a touring artist and as a choreographer conducting place-based performance research at a number of international sites,[2] it makes sense that a single performer or a single group, working with a shared technical core, could move from site to site creating what she refers to as a "field of research" that is about each specific place while at the same time existing "between" all of those places. Tess' understanding of place-based

---

[1] From here on, "De Quincey", "De Quincey Co" and "DQCo" refer to the De Quincey Company and "de Quincey" or "Tess" refers to Tess de Quincey.

[2] Most notably, Tess has long-term connections with locations in Japan, India and Denmark.

knowledge acquisition, in this way, is both specific – at times even site-microscopic – while at the same time being relational or associative. She denies neither frame but, rather, tends to articulate how intimate knowledge of one place can inform – or at least lead to – understanding of another place. In this sense, place-based knowledge acquisition for de Quincey can be understood, narratively and pragmatically, as a journey.

Speaking to a mixed group of academics and performance practitioners in the well-known Sydney venue Performance Space in 2006, Tess explained her long time creative attraction to the "Centre" – the Australian Central Desert – as being inherently linked to her fascination with the continent of Australia. On this day, she was speaking as part of a panel that had been assembled by the editors of the Australian arts journal *RealTime*, on the topic of "practice research". It was approximately one year after she and her team of collaborators had returned from their residency in Alice Springs, following the production of *Dictionary of Atmospheres*.

De Quincey was particularly well chosen for this panel on the topic of practice research. Her work in the Australian Central Desert, 1999-2005, represents a form of performance-as-research that has consistently attracted the attention of Australian and international performance practitioners and scholars.[3] Furthermore, de Quincey's work has been substantially influenced by her long-term collaboration with the Department of Performance Studies (DPS) at the University of Sydney, through which the University has provided de Quincey's projects with funding and infrastructural support in exchange for the opportunity to document and analyze De Quincey Co rehearsals and performances as part of the undergraduate and postgraduate curriculum.

The unique collaboration between de Quincey and the DPS crystallized around the organization of the three Triple Alice art-labs. These art-labs, referred to as Triple Alice 1, 2 and 3 (alternatively referred to as TA1, TA2 and TA3),[4] represent a fertile period in the formation of the De Quincey Co and the DPS alike. Performance Studies at Sydney[5] is organized on a rehearsal studies model of pedagogy and research, unlike any other perfor-

---

[3] The Triple Alice laboratories had international participation each year. The *Dictionary of Atmospheres* team had three international contributors.

[4] I will use "Triple Alice 1" (or TA1), etc. and "BodyWeather," but these words are configured differently by other authors. When quoting, I have tried to retain each author's unique configuration of these words.

[5] The University of Sydney may be referred to, alternately, as "Sydney" or "USyd."

mance studies program in the world (Maxwell 2006). In Tess de Quincey, scholars at Sydney had found an artist creating work of significant interest to faculty members as well as to students. Collaboration on the Triple Alice projects has produced theses on the Honours, Master's and PhD levels and resulted in numerous articles and several publications edited by DPS founder Gay McAuley, as well as the ongoing interdisciplinary research group known as the Place and Performance Seminar which produced the book *Unstable Ground: Performance and the Politics of Place* (2006). In the DPS, de Quincey had not only found an academic home and a network of support, but also a stimulating group of scholar-practitioners who would come, over time, to exert a degree of influence on her methods of making and understanding her own performances. It is fair to say that, over the last ten-plus years of collaboration, Tess de Quincey and the Department of Performance Studies at the University of Sydney have produced each other in certain key ontological respects.

Triple Alice Engagement

> TripleAlice engages the space of the Central Desert of Australia as fundamental to its mapping of practice – an environment of artistic, cultural and media exchange. Aiming to be held annually, TripleAlice convenes a forum and a series of lives, site- and temporally-specific laboratories staged each year in 'the Centre.' Envisaged in stages, concentric circles of artistic and cultural exchange build out in ripples from the centre to establish interchange with artists around the periphery of Australia to then engage with international artists, scientists & thinkers. The forum and laboratories are accessible through an interactive website which is formative of, and integral to, the event. (de Quincey 2003: 25)

In her article, "BodyWeather in the Central Desert of Australia," DPS founder Gay McAuley records Tess de Quincey as stating that her creative practice seeks to train artists to "empathise on a cellular level" with aspects of the physical geography of specific environments (McAuley 2000: 5). English-born, De Quincey's primary professional identification is as a practitioner of the Japanese contemporary dance form BodyWeather. She lived, trained and performed with Min Tanaka's Mai Juku BodyWeather company in Japan for six years (1985-1991) and subsequently practiced and performed as a

BodyWeather artist in Denmark before moving permanently to Australia in 1998 and starting her own company in 2000. Tanaka created his BodyWeather farm and performance training method in order to distance himself from Tatsumi Hijikata and create his own trajectory (Bergmark 1991; De Quincey 2011; Viala and Masson-Sekine 1988; Stein and Tanaka 1986; Tanaka 1986).[6] BodyWeather is thus understood to be a form that is an aesthetic and conceptual relative of Butoh, and so part of a lineage of contemporary movement practices in Japan that were initiated after World War II and have since become diasporic forms with highly varied manifestations, particularly in Australia, North America and Europe.

BodyWeather training must be understood as operating quite distinctly and separately from Butoh training. Although both BodyWeather and Butoh devote pedagogical attention towards environmental receptivity, the role of place and the natural world is much more strongly appreciated in Body-Weather. While "Butoh training in Japan places images within the body and … then explores the imagination and its surreal capacities", BodyWeather training is more specifically organized around environmental engagement and the experience of nature (De Quincey 2011). Stuart Grant, who was a student at the DPS when he studied with Tess and has since gone on to collaborate with her professionally, writes that "[f]or Min Tanaka, the founder of Bodyweather, dancing is an ontology of the identity of self and place" (Grant with de Quincey 2006: 247). In fact, it is a "self/place" that factors strongly in BodyWeather training.

From its origins with Tanaka, BodyWeather was organized within the context of a communal living environment on a farm. Part of the training for Tess while she was a member of Tanaka's Mai Juku company, living on the BodyWeather farm, involved labor on the farm. This is the case for anyone who wishes to study with Tanaka, as training is not a matter of art practice that is incidentally carried out on a farm, but rather art practice that includes the tending of crops and the maintenance of facilities to help run a farm. In many respects, understanding de Quincey's engagement in the Triple Alice art-laboratories (as a way of understanding *Dictionary of Atmospheres*) must take into account an appreciation of the very specific kind of training environment that she experienced on Min Tanaka's BodyWeather farm. Training

---

[6] In email correspondence from Tess, she writes that Tanaka "distanced himself from Hijikata because he didn't want to be swallowed up by him and in following his own trajectory he developed Bodyweather" (de Quincey 2011).

as a dancer with Mai Juku was not exclusively training in a form related to Butoh (as Butoh now refers to a number of different kinds of training practices from a number of different international sites), and not just in communal farm living, but training in a Japanese cultural practice. Tess is aware of the significant differences that exist between BodyWeather in the Japanese context and BodyWeather in the Australian context:

> [Tess] explains that when Japanese students first enter into a practice, they make the decision to 'give themselves' to the process. They realize that there will be many things that they will not understand, but that does not matter, for they carry a *trust* in a number of factors. Firstly, they hold a trust in a *Master/Teacher* figure…Secondly…the Japanese student trusts in the *process* itself … The third element of the learning process in which a Japanese student has complete trust is *time*. (Dunn 2003: 38)

Tess' description of the nature of trust in the *Master/Teacher*, in the *process* and in *time* in the Japanese student context is in keeping with Barbara Sellers-Young's observations of the teacher/student relationship in another form of Japanese dance, Nihon Buyo. Sellers-Young explains how the trust that students place in the Master/Teacher serves a specific function when she writes that "[t]here is an assumption that the student will not only learn the form but will be transformed psychologically as well" (1993: 10). While the Australian participants in Triple Alice were less inclined to automatically "give themselves" to the BodyWeather training and the BodyWeather communal context, as Sarah Dunn suggests, in the same way that Tess says that Japanese students would, the Triple Alice laboratories are a space in which, over a period of weeks, participants can begin to learn what it might look like, feel like and mean – psychologically, culturally, and ontologically – to "give themselves" to the process.

The passage of time was significant to the Triple Alice project. Not only did the laboratories involve a three-week-long intensive commitment from participants, the project was designed to occur annually. McAuley writes that de Quincey had "planned from the outset that the project would extend over a number of years, three at least" (McAuley 2003: vii). Duration was also a factor in the actual exercises used in the Triple Alice BodyWeather training. Grant describes three exercises that encapsulate key elements of the training:

- "Bisoku", in which participants walk in the sand at 1mm/1sec
- "Omnicentral Imaging", in which "the body is divided into four areas" and each area moves at different speeds and with different weights and images attached
- "Ground-Being", in which participants concentrate "on one small patch of sand, observing the changing shapes, speeds, and directions in its micro-topography, the mounds, the divots and holes, each grain, the spaces between the grains, taking the texture of it into our bodies". (Grant with de Quincey 2006: 249-51)

The objective, as Grant describes it, is "the body becoming place" (Grant with de Quincey 2006: 251). In the Triple Alice laboratories, the training involved very much an attempt to get participants to feel *in* and *of* a place – even if only for a handful of weeks at a time. This was established substantially through ritual activities and repetition of exercises – hence, the added significance of a repetition from year to year – all of which was organized around a highly regimented schedule. "The structure of the training was generally repeated each day in order to 'aid the observation of change'" (Dunn 2003: 24).

The exercises that Grant describes – training for sensitivity and receptivity accomplished through a kind of dissociation from the everyday or pedestrian body – are part of the "Groundwork", which is only one part of the daily physical training. Six days of each week at Triple Alice involved at least two hours of rigorous, continuous calisthenics performed outdoors followed by another two hours of stretching and flexibility exercises. Tina Harrison, who trained as a student in the DPS at the University of Sydney and subsequently trained and danced with Tess for several years as part of the De Quincey Co, described the Triple Alice schedule in the following way:

> A typical day began with a very early breakfast to accommodate an adequate time for digestion before the two-hour Muscle and Bone (MB) workout … then onto Manipulations, which is work with a partner, focusing on aligning, stretching and relaxing the body … After this, it was… light lunch and a moment of rest … chores … [and] the afternoon session was the Groundwork … developing sensitivity, awareness and scope of expression through the body… (Harrison 2003: 15)

Participants' time was carefully managed; even those entering the process with questions about the function of the training or the intentions of the instructor were very quickly enfolded into the rhythm and consciousness of the schedule. Thus, one of the key distinctions in the translation of BodyWeather practices from the Japanese/Tanaka context to the Australian/de Quincey context was that while participants did not enter the laboratory environment with the automatic deference, respect and trust in the Master/Teacher and the process, because Australian participants do have a respect and a trust in a schedule, deference to the *schedule* became, perhaps, a way in to deference for the Master/Teacher and the process.

Triple Alice activities were carried out as a group and yet there was also substantial attention toward individual experience at every stage:

> Each participant was complicit in the framing of his perception of an experience. Every person experienced each moment from a solitary place in space; thus there were as many different viewpoints at any moment in time as there were people. (Dunn 2003: 35)

While the schedule was organized around repeated group encounters and activities, the training, as Tess delivered it, incorporated a substantial emphasis on journaling, note-taking and other forms of personal reflection designed to aid individual participants in charting their own, personal experiences. Tina Harrison describes the scene when she arrived on the first day of Triple Alice 1:

> Down on the riverbed a group of about 40 participants gathered around Tess, listening to her instructions for the next Groundwork exercise and then rushed past me to get notebooks and pens. (Harrison 2003: 14)

There are at least two ways to understand this behavior. Firstly, the rush to get notebooks and pens is a mark of the impact of the DPS affiliation, and the extent to which that affiliation has been productive of the De Quincey training process in Australia. Secondly, intertwined with the DPS affiliation, the rush to get notebooks and pens can be understood as a tactical outcome of Tess' modification of a Japanese training system to adapt to an Australian sensibility.

The way that adaptation manifested in the Triple Alice context can be partly understood through a description of the nature of Performance Studies at Sydney. As Ian Maxwell writes in his article "Performance Studies at the University of Sydney" (2006), the DPS has a unique history of methodological exploration, much of which was envisioned and pioneered by Gay McAuley. From the outset, DPS explored aspects of performance documentation and for a long while its methods were influenced by both semiotics and ethnography. Eventually the staff collectively landed on what became their unique "rehearsal studies" model for analyzing performance practices, in which professional groups – most of whom are based in or rehearsing for a show in Sydney – are invited to rehearse in the Department's Rex Cramphorn Studio so that students and faculty might study and theorize how performance groups make work. Tess de Quincey has consistently received support from DPS through this program and by the time Triple Alice 1 was in the development stages for 1999, the DPS was already a strong presence in the life of what would become the De Quincey Company, with Sydney students matriculating and going on to become Company members and collaborators.

Thus, to return to McAuley's recording of Tess' training objective being one of "empathizing on a cellular level", it is significant to understand that this statement is coming from a practitioner whose work has been archived by a single, dedicated academic program for well over a decade. "Empathizing on a cellular level" suggests that the de Quincey BodyWeather practice – and in this case, the work carried out in the Triple Alice project – is capable of training artists to establish an emotional relationship with a particular aspect of the physical geography within a site that is at work on the most fundamental – the cellular – level. This is a rather provocative suggestion – a suggestion that this creative practice is art and science combined, that it enacts an essential change within the practitioner and that it provides a platform for an emotional kinship between human and site.

Such claims are part of the basis for the ongoing DPS fascination with de Quincey and her approach to creative work. The DPS rehearsal studies model, which employs ethnographic methodologies and carefully choreographed modes of documentation, fastidiously records and archives creative processes. Creative processes that actively incorporate documentation within the act of rehearsal and production would be all the more at home within this rehearsal studies model of analysis. It would be difficult to pinpoint exactly when Tess began to document, to archive her own work as she does currently, but it is fair to say that the nature of her documentation – the quantity of the documentation and the qualities of the narratives that emerge within the documentation – have been substantially influenced by being looked at and being partially produced by the DPS.

Analysis of the participant journals and performance documentation that has emerged from the Triple Alice laboratories reveals that de Quincey has had to modify her own embodied interpretation of BodyWeather as she studied it in Japan, in order to make the training comprehensible for Australian artists. Particularly after her 1991 laboratory with Australian performers at Lake Mungo, there was a recognition that aspects of BodyWeather as she had practiced it in Japan would not work effectively in Australia. When participant-observer Sarah Dunn writes that "over the last ten years since leaving Japan, Tess has been 'refining' the form" (2003: 38), she is explaining how Tess has endeavored to make BodyWeather more accessible in the Australian context.

One of the aspects that had to be transformed was the means of communication. According to De Quincey Co members, many of whom have studied not only with Tess but also with Min Tanaka in Japan, Tess' version of BodyWeather today includes much more discussion; and with discussion comes notes. The translation of BodyWeather from the Japanese to the Australian context was one in which the spoken and written word featured much more prominently, and this was ideally suited to the DPS interest in and dependence on documentation. Whether or not this specific aspect of adaptation is coincidental, the adaptation of de Quincey's BodyWeather process to the Australian context can be understood as having been developed like a double helix – one strand running as the translation of BodyWeather from the Japanese to the Australian context, the second, intertwined strand running as the influence of the developing research agenda of the DPS at the University of Sydney.

It is important to keep in mind, however, that there is a built-in assumption about the possibilities for translation that exist within the logic of BodyWeather as a form. While it is not surprising that "there are problems associated with bringing a training system from one culture to another", Min Tanaka "initially developed BodyWeather as a 'dialogue between East and West,' so presumably within the initial structure, there lay cross-cultural potential" (Dunn 2003: 38). But what does that mean: "cross-cultural potential"? In this case, the training is perceived to be a vehicle for translation, with endlessly expansive applications.

Tess takes the argument one step further when she posits that Body-Weather is not just about translation "between" cultures, but that it has the power to connect students to something even more essential than culture:

> [Tess] prefers to look at it as a *sub*-cultural phenomenon, believing that the experience of Bodyweather allows people from different cultures to recognize something that is 'below' culture: 'As a process of self-observation it engenders a capacity to begin to see where culture begins and ends.' (Dunn 2003: 38)

Maintaining the tension between the process and experience of the "self" and the process and experience of the "group" is another aspect of Tess' translation that, like the Triple Alice schedule, works its effects subtly. With the structure of the schedule, Australian and other international participants who would not otherwise be inclined to "give themselves" over to the Body-Weather process and to an unquestioning trust in the Master/Teacher, are brought, over a period of time, to "give themselves" to the schedule. By default, the process of giving in to the schedule or, rather, giving one's full attention to the schedule, leads to an implicit trust in the Master/Teacher and in the role that duration plays in the deepening of the practice. Similarly, the effective maintenance of the focus on "self" through practices of "self-observation" is managed largely through the hyper-documentation as it exists within the Triple Alice environment. Illustrations of this dedication to processes of documentation abound in the published works on Triple Alice – there is Tina Harrison's aforementioned recording of *40 participants gathered around Tess, listening to her instructions for the next Groundwork exercise and then rushed past me to get notebooks and pens*; Sarah Dunn's article describes the project's designated "documenters, whose job it was to frame the bodies of the participants within the landscape" (2003: 35); as well as Ian Maxwell's account of "close descriptions of inner bodily states and sensations as everyone tunes in to the minutiae of their internal landscapes" (2003: 70). These processes of documentation ultimately engender in participants a willingness to engage in group behaviors and, over time, generate a group "sense" that the collective is in agreement about what is happening because all individuals are collectively participating in what is happening. Through the self, participants find the group. Through action, the collective is rcified.

Group numbers and group identities and sub-identities factor in strongly in the Triple Alice experiences and in the writing that emerges out of the experiences. At Triple Alice 3:

> There were forty-four participants: four performance studies aca-
> demics, one anthropologist, one historian, one ethnobotanist, one
> virologist, two administrators, two technical documenters, one di-
> rector, fourteen performers, eight Indigenous artists, and nine
> sound, visual and installation artists. (Grant with de Quincey
> 2006: 255)

There is a kind of giddiness in all of these numbers and descriptors. Prior to reading Grant's description of the scene, there is only a kind of generalized sense that an amorphous "group" gathered at Hamilton Downs for three weeks to carry out a rigorous and introspective set of physical exercises and experiments. Through Grant's numbers and descriptors, we are provided with texture – the texture that is generated from numbers and *titles*. His list establishes authority, and he is not alone with the listing. Lists appear in almost all of the descriptions that have emerged out of the Triple Alice experience. With all of those *different people* performing all of those *different roles*, how could you not make a list? And, further, in an environment textured by a set of literal ethnographic lenses set in place to capture moment to moment, place to place, move to move, the list seems inevitable.

There is an impressive attention to names and roles and numbers in Triple Alice and yet, "[m]aybe surprisingly, maybe not, at *Triple Alice 3* we had very little contact with the traditional owners[7] and very scant instruction in the stories of the place" (Grant with de Quincey 2006: 254). Grant finds this surprising because Tess describes the Triple Alice project as being about "'the confronting heartbeat of the continent'" (de Quincey in Grant with de Quincey 2006: 247) and the confrontation presumably has much to do with aspects of traditional ownership. Yet this observation of the paucity of contact with the traditional owners and the scant instruction in the stories of the

---

[7] The phrase "traditional owners" refers to the Aboriginal group that is recognized as having the primary "traditional" (before settlement) relationship with a particular location or region. Often ceremonies, political events, and academic conferences in Australia begin with a "Welcome to Country" delivered by the "traditional owners" of the place in which the event is occurring. What this means is that one or more individuals affiliated with the Aboriginal group that is recognized as having the primary "traditional" relationship with that place/area/location, will deliver an address and formally recognize the event as having been approved to take place by the traditional owners. It is a mark of respect for Aboriginal culture when a group seeks permission to hold an event in a particular location by inviting the traditional owners to deliver a Welcome to Country speech.

place, from the perspectives of the traditional owners, might be considered to be reasonable in the context of de Quincey's BodyWeather training environment. While de Quincey consistently demonstrates both her respect for the stories and knowledge of the traditional owners, and while she and De Quincey Co members conduct substantial research into the cultural histories of particular places, her site-specific orientation to her creative practice is not limited by pre-existing narratives of place. Secondly, as de Quincey is trying to train performing/artists to accumulate information about an environment, while she acknowledges that the Central Desert environment is highly political and historically complex, the political and the historical are understood to be two of the hundreds – thousands – of factors about the environment that might be taken into account in the explorations, and not necessarily more or less important. As Tess has organized the training, each individual has to find her own way through the process – establish her own narrative. While some participants were more drawn to particular aspects regarding the history of the place, others did not crave this information. In either respect, the Body-Weather training as Tess administers it places emphasis on *what is happening in an individual body*. The truth or fact or significance of an aspect of a history of place is only important primarily to the extent that it is processed through an individual body.

The training posits, philosophically and epistemologically, that it helps bodies become more receptive. However, the training – at least in the Triple Alice context – is not as concerned with managing the particularities of what those bodies receive or how each individual processes what she receives. Sarah Dunn recalls that her experience in Triple Alice 1 was marked by "the re-emergence of many memories from my past" (2003: 44). Dunn says that these memories "had no seeming relation to the activities" in which she was participating, that "they came from everywhere", that they were "ordinary" and that she "had no conscious control" of what she remembered (2003: 44). This kind of process – the processing of an individual process – is what is of interest in the BodyWeather training carried out in the Triple Alice laboratories, "with the intention of expanding our consciousness … drawing us closer to what has long been considered a 'primitive' way of apprehending the world" (Dunn 2003: 45). Once again, Dunn expresses an aspect of the training as it relates to *individual* consciousness, but the argument then goes that *through* this individualized process, participants can hope to connect to some collective way of being in the world. This connects back to Tess' argument that BodyWeather is interested in sub-culture, which, in this case, is that state or sensibility that happens *before* culture. Even though de Quincey's creative work is not preoccupied with or stymied by pre-existing narratives – historical or cultural otherwise – with regard to the sites in which she practices her training regimen, when she discusses the function of the training, she cannot help but be roped back into a set of narrative devices that depend on temporal and cultural distinctions.

We can see in Dunn's own narrative that, though the training is meant to take participants out of context and disorient them with the objective being to re-program and change the "topography of self" (Dunn 2003: 44), participants are not immune to the narratives that are already operating in all aspects of their reception and analysis of the training. They cannot eradicate what they have been taught and have come to know about this place. While de Quincey's BodyWeather training does not claim to affect – or want to affect – such changes (Tess does not express desire to be responsible for rectifying the myths of place), there is an implicit *sense* in the writings of participants that this is the power that the training holds. Senior De Quincey Co member Peter Fraser writes during TA1: "As usual surprised at how much I can respond to nature in body weather context" (Fraser 1999). The power of the training, here again, is articulated in terms of a useful disorientation, a cleansing re-programming that involves a dis-engagement with city life and the implements and influences of Western/city/contemporary thinking.[8] Company member Victoria Hunt writes during Triple Alice 1:

> Buried in the creekbed, feelings came, memories of walking through monkey forest ... coming to a peaceful understanding of fear. Throbbing life. Held by something profoundly maternal. I wanted to lie there for a very very long time, accepting the memories which map my existence. I felt annoyed to have a wrist watch marking a crude boundary against my time. (Hunt 1999)

In the words of participants describing their reception of the training and its effects on their reception of place, there is a sense of the bucolic, the vulnerable, even the innocent. But these sentiments belie a set of unquestioned assumptions that are all the more curious given the group's reluctance to

---

[8] That said, Tess clarifies that Bodyweather "does not set out to dissociate or deprogramme pedestrian movements" per se, "but instead values these intrinsic everyday movements to mine into them and explore the underlying subconscious aspect of them" (de Quincey 2011).

gesture towards any claim that their work is explicitly inter-cultural. In Tess' own reckoning about her practice, the "emphasis on the subcultural is to … understand more about what inhabiting a cultural pattern, with all its distinctions, means in a more deep sense" (de Quincey 2011). With adequate training and investment in the process, a participant can, with increasing depth, inhabit a specific cultural location, while allowing the perception of that cultural location to be embroidered, modified, complemented and estranged by the fine details of place.

Part of inviting the fine details of the Central Desert-as-place to flood the training environment manifests in Tess' "enormous efforts to gather a great deal of information and people who could give insight into their wealth of experience from a great variety of backgrounds" (de Quincey 2011). Triple Alice 3 featured a range of guest speakers, including:

- anthropologist Scott Campbell-Smith who gave a "campfire account of his travels in the area"
- Peter Latz, who led the group "through a well-rehearsed walking tour of the bush tucker in the area"
- historian Dick Kimber, who engaged the group with a "discussion of whether or not the dispossession of the peoples of Central Australia constituted a genocide"
- Steve, the traditional owner, who showed the group "how to cook rootails in the fire"
- local artist Anne Mosey, who talked about her "hard-won relationships with the Aborigines in the area" and
- Dorothy Napangardi and a group of Warlpiri women artists from Yuendumu and Nyirippi who "did some painting" and "showed…some dances" (Grant with de Quincey 2006: 254)[9]

Here is another important list, one which helps to demonstrate that Triple Alice is a project with a stated objective being to "'hothouse a wide range of conceptual, cultural and critical issues'" (Grant with de Quincey 2006: 255). And that "hothouse" term is particularly important in understanding how, for instance, all of these special presentations factored into the de Quincey ac-

---

[9] The full list of contributors is substantially longer than this – this list represents only an abbreviated account from one of the labs – TA3.

counting system. While Tess is not conducting a systematic inventory of the cultural and historical narratives of this specific place, she is interested in creating an accumulation, a critical mass of bodies and interests and information. In this kind of "hothouse" environment, it is the *experience* of the hothouse, the *experience* of the accumulation that *is* the burning point, and nowhere is this more evident than in the Triple Alice campfire experiences. Most every guest presentation involved a campfire that either accompanied the presentation or was *part of* the presentation. The campfire was the literal place where bodies could gather and recognize the act the gathering. The campfire was also a means by which exchange could happen.

The campfires were emblematic of the sentiment of the whole Triple Alice enterprise, as they were organized around a set of group rituals that were of equal and interrelated importance to the individual investigations. Tina Harrison recalls, for instance, that Triple Alice 3 "again…began with a performative offering" in which "[c]ampfires were lit, kangaroo tails were cooked, and we sat around and ate, talked, laughed and looked at the skies" (2003: 18). Viewing the many hours of video footage of the Triple Alice projects that are stored in the archives of the DPS, one can observe that campfires feature prominently in the Triple Alice documentation, pointing to the desire and intent of the Triple Alice project: to create a forum for exchange. Yes, the training is about receptivity – but a receptivity that is established in order to more effectively create an exchange. Yes, the schedule is regimented and incorporates group activities with intensive personal reflection – but all of this is carried out as a means to an end. The point *is* the exchange.

While all of the guest presentations during the Triple Alice experiences were valued and integrated among the rest of the training, perhaps the most significant visit was that of Aboriginal artist Dorothy Napangardi. Part of the idea, or the "dreaming" for the laboratories that both Tess de Quincey and Gay McAuley admit was "wildly ambitious" was "the intention to make contact with members of the Indigenous community living at Yuendumu[10] and to explore the possibilities of a genuine exchange between different performance traditions grounded in experience of place" (McAuley 2003: vii). Again, Tess expresses the means by which a singular, individual experience of contact might translate out into a much larger "net" of systems. In this case, a single point of encounter between Triple Alice participants and Doro-

---

[10] Yuendumu is an Aboriginal community located 293km northwest of Alice Springs.

thy Napangardi – who brought her "aunties", members of her extended family from her community, along with her – could provide for a meaningful exchange that could lead to a limitless exchange among a wide variety of *traditions grounded in the experience of place*. This must not be mistaken for tokenism, in which Tess, out of some sense of responsibility, is merely ticking off a box entitled "Aboriginal encounter". Rather, this is a singular encounter that Tess reckons will be a part of and also stand in for a whole cosmology of encounters across difference.

And so the "pendulations" that Tess invokes in her description of her own research are not just between the city and the desert, not just between long and short, and not just between fast and slow. The training pendulates between broad and fine brush strokes – between exercises that Tess claims can engender the "capacity to begin to see where culture begins and ends" and the micro-topographical intimacy generated between a dancer and *one small patch of sand*. The circles of attention pendulate between the group and the individual – the experience of staying in time with a group of 44 others all jumping and leaping and stretching together for two hours continuously, followed by the experience of quiet, meditative notet-aking in a private, personal journal. The through-line, the thing that holds it all together is the list-making:

- the number of people who attended
- their names
- their occupations
- where they are from
- their role in the context of the lab
- the e-journal entries of every participant on every day that they attended the laboratory

Everything is transposed – from body to page, from page to body, from body to dry-erase board, from dry-erase board to body, from body to body, from body to sand, from sand to body to…. Not surprisingly, these transpositions, these pendulations, produce the "somatic status of being shaken up" (Dunn 2003: 44). Yet it is the *somatic status of being shaken up* that participants describe as a way to elucidate the use-value of the training – as a way, even, to describe the larger social and cultural significance of the training.

Triple Alice Ontology

More than a few have expressed the difficulty in writing about the Triple Alice experience. Ian Maxwell searches for answers years after his experience at Triple Alice 3 when he writes: "How might one write about this experience? A sociology of a (rather extreme) artists' colony? A performance analysis? An ethnography? A phenomenology?" (Maxwell 2003: 67). Maxwell paraphrases the argument in Peter Snow's PhD thesis (2002) – written largely in response to Snow's participation in the Triple Alice laboratories – when he writes:

> [D]eep in the heart of the practice, TripleAlice was about … the practice itself, not the 'big picture' questions … not those of critiques of culture, of national identity, of ownership and politics, but those of ontology: fundamental philosophical questions as to the nature of our being(s), best explored by means of a rigorous, if blinkered, attention to one's dilated self. (Maxwell 2003: 71).

But McAuley insists that engagement at this ontological level *is necessarily also* engagement on the social and political levels. McAuley points out that:

> even if it can be maintained that Body Weather as a practice is concerned with ontological rather than social and political issues, I would wish to argue that a profound shift in ontological awareness is what is required if we are to confront the human and ecological legacies of our colonial past. (McAuley 2003: xi)

For McAuley, the value of the Triple Alice/BodyWeather experience was that it promised engagement with the kind of fundamental ontological questioning that is necessary *in order to* confront the nation's colonial past.

For Stuart Grant, it is always both, or, one in the same. "As an ongoing response within Triple Alice," Grant is concerned with "perform[ing] the practice of Bodyweather to learn how to live better in this country" as an "answer to an ethical question" (Grant with de Quincey 2006: 249). Grant echoes McAuley's sentiment that the BodyWeather work of Tess de Quincey and her collaborators "can contribute to the profoundly important question of how to live responsibly in this place" (McAuley 2006: 22), when he explains that BodyWeather involves his own "very personal story" related to how "to

live this place, my country, as responsibly and as responsively as I am able"
(Grant with de Quincey 2006: 249).

What does it mean to *live better* in a place, or, *live more responsibly*?
Why would this be so important for Triple Alice participants? And, what is
the relationship between being "shaken up somatically" and learning to live
more responsibly? A few participants specifically articulate a sense of how
the Triple Alice experience has contributed to their learning to "live better"
or "more responsibly" by narrating a trajectory from perceptions of the desert
as the "vast unknown" to experiences of love and intimacy with the desert.
Kristina Harrison made her first trip to the Central Desert as a University of
Sydney DPS student assigned the privilege of documenting Triple Alice 1 in
1999. Harrison subsequently wrote her Honours casebook on Triple Alice 1
and continued to train and dance with Tess as a member of the De Quincey
Company from 2001-2005. In 2003, having attended all of the Triple Alice
laboratories and having taken on increasing leadership responsibilities within
the laboratory training regimen, she reflects on that first trip:

> [R]emembering fragments of primary and high school colonial
> Australia history, I equipped myself with romantic, red earthed,
> exotic dreams of a Bohemian experience in the heart of my home-
> land. Boy, was I in for a shock! Walking out of Alice Springs air-
> port just four hours after leaving what was a cool, brisk Sydney
> morning, I was blinded by the extremely penetrating sun, which
> was already gnawing at my skin, as was too the blanket of flies.
> The land was a deep orange red and the trees were bare, black and
> scarred, fitting so far the image of the desert that I had brought
> with me. As we drove out of town towards Hamilton Downs, an
> old abandoned cattle station *cum* youth camp where we were stay-
> ing, the vegetation became wilder and the prominence of the sky,
> its colour and contrast to the earth left me awestruck. (Harrison
> 2003: 14)

Tracing her own shifting responses to the land from 1999-2001, Kristina
expresses how the feelings of "shock" and "awe" in 1999 turned to feelings
of being "embraced by the land" (2003: 16) in 2000 and then to sentiments of
"knowing" (2003: 18) specific aspects of the physical geography of the land
in 2001. Through personal and group rituals carried out each year, aspects of
repetition within each lab facilitated, for Tina, the transition from the "shock"
of the desert's environmental challenges to the "known" of a landscape with
which she felt a strong attachment. Tina makes a point, for instance, to return

to a particular riverbed location in Triple Alice 3 with which she had bonded in Triple Alice 2, explaining that "[c]oming back to Hamilton Downs for the third time felt so familiar that I plunged my body deep into the riverbed and slept" (2003: 18). Through each individual's experience of return and repetition, there is a perception of a learning process and a growth, as Tina notes her "somewhat blinded" perception of years past had been replaced by a responsibility that would "not allow for mishaps of any sort" (2003: 18). Tina's narration of her journey from "shock" to "intimacy", from "blindness" to "responsibility" comes closest of all the Triple Alice narratives to a direct engagement between personal transformation and problematic aspects of the Australian history of settlement.

It is difficult to determine why the analyses of the Triple Alice project so seldomly engage specifically with aspects of the history of settlement and matters of Aboriginality. In some cases, perhaps the author assumes a primarily Australian readership and so there is not a perceived need to rehash aspects of history that would be presumed common knowledge. In other cases, the author needs room to really explore aspects of the BodyWeather training or the effects of the desert environment. There really is so much to write about in these laboratories. Yet another possibility for this absence is that Tess herself does not spend a great deal of time speaking specifically about these things. As many of the analysts are trained ethnographers, perhaps they do not engage specifically with matters of history because their subjects – Tess and her collaborators – do not engage specifically with matters of history. Stuart Grant does ask "what Bodyweather and traditional Aboriginal culture might have in common" and how he, himself, "might learn to live with the knowledge of and attempt to play some part in the stopping of the still continuing cultural genocide on which this country stands" (Grant with de Quincey 2006: 262). That's pretty specific. But Grant quickly explains that he hasn't answered these questions and that he still doesn't "know how to live comfortably in the only place on earth which feels like home to me" (Grant with de Quincey 2006: 263). Grant's direct engagement with these questions, however, is built within a piece of writing that he developed with de Quincey, herself, and further, the essay took as its task explaining a number of different facets of the Triple Alice project's engagement with place. There was not a great deal of room for Grant to explore in detail his own connection between the personal, the political and the historical.

I would like to propose that there is another reason why the specific histories of Australian settlement are not engaged. I think engagement with the specifics of these histories might not only be difficult – emotionally, personally; I think engagement with the specifics of the history might disrupt certain aspects of the narrative that participants have developed about "Triple Alice being about itself", and "Bodyweather being about ontology". I do not deny that Triple Alice is about itself. And I do not deny that BodyWeather does engage with questions about ontology. However, aspects of these stories about BodyWeather conceal conflicts that are inherent in the *doing* of BodyWeather in specific places. It is my sense that a bit of engagement with the historical might reveal a new level of significance of the work – a level that has only revealed itself thus far through the disjunctures produced in the transporting, translating, and transposing of Triple Alice practices into the Todd-Mpartntwe riverbed.

Latent Histories Informing Triple Alice Transformations

From the colonial perspective, "nature" in Australia was seen – at first – as a vast museum or storehouse and, subsequently, as a foe. The Romantic revolution, as a reaction against rationalism, working in conversation with the project of colonial acquisition, sought out in nature the sublime as cathartic and therapeutic, with a focus on the intimate connection to the solitary experience of the "wild". In the understanding of nature in and of Australia, the Australian desert came, over time, to serve a significant function in establishing what was "wild" and where "wild" was located.

While the history of "wilderness" in Australia is only slightly over 100 years old, the history of the unknown with regard to Australia is significant in what would come to be understood as wilderness in the Australian context. The history of the Australian continent as a relative unknown is informed by a European desire to create systems of nomenclature. The Greek language provided the first nomenclature utilized by European colonizers that confirmed the as-of-yet undiscovered land mass (*Terra*) based on its presupposed location in the south (*Australis*) and content, which was unknown (*Incognita*). These words alone ascribed on the continent and the histories that would spring from those names the qualities that would define its early parameters. Jumping forward in time, the first colonial encounters at Botany Bay in the 1770 Sydney Harbour landing aimed, in large part, to facilitate a botanical expedition. These histories of naming not only reflect the systems of domination and the philosophies of domination that were part of the colonial enterprise, but illustrate how these naming systems, themselves, are systems of domination.

Around 150 AD Ptolemy made a map of the entire world, including that which was "known" from a European perspective and that which had yet to be captured beyond their imagination:

> Because Greek standards of symmetry demanded land in the far south to balance that known in the northern hemisphere, Ptolemy invented a vast continent south of the equator. Belief in the *necessary existence* of a southern land mass persisted for many hundreds of years. During the sixteenth and seventeenth centuries Renaissance cartographers drew the land boundaries for a continent in the south temperate zone and affixed the name *Terra Australis Incognita* – the unknown south land … European certainty of the existence of *Terra Australis* points to the durability of prejudice and myth, while the provisional *Incognita* reveals an ethnocentric arrogance towards the non-European world. Countries remained unknown only until European discovery and possession ripped away their concealing marks. (Lines 1991: 15)

As the Greeks needed a southern continent on their maps to balance the known land mass in the northern hemisphere, so the notion of consciousness relies on the necessary existence of the subconscious or unconscious. *Terra Australis Incognita* reliably encompasses both geometry and psychology at once, as the great, deep suppressed unknown lives beneath the active conscious mind, which is perceived to be "known".

Robert Hughes writes that this logic was carried forward to England's population during the Australian colonial project. Largely removed from the world of letters and news up through the mid 19th century, it is easy to understand how a kind of pre-modern sensibility towards the southern continent could be maintained:

> It made sense, of a kind, to assume that the further south one went, the more grotesque life would become. What demonic freaks, what affronts to normality, might the Southern Continent not produce? And what trials for the mariner? Waterspouts, hurricanes, clouds of darkness at midday, ship-eating whales, islands that saw and had tusks – this imagined country was perhaps infernal, its landscape that of Hell itself. Within its inscrutable other-

> ness, every fantasy could be contained; it was the geographical
> unconscious. So there was a deep, ironic resonance in the way the
> British, having brought the Pacific at last into the realm of Euro-
> pean consciousness, having explored and mapped it, promptly
> demonized Australia once more by chaining their criminals on its
> innocent dry coast. It was to become the continent of sin. (Hughes
> 1987: 44)

It was as if the very naming system which had organized Australia as a stand-in for the subconscious had somehow managed to maintain the *Incognita* aspect of the continent purposefully. And yet, even as convicts were sent over as part of an extraordinary removal of European "waste" to the unknown and unseen, the colonial enterprise persisted in carrying out systems by which colonizers could "know" the continent on its own terms – through botanical classification.

British colonial presence in Australia was at the outset interested in collecting botanical information. By the 19th century, the British Empire was embroiled in the process of replicating entire regions, as the European colonial project attempted to propagate "new Europes" elsewhere on the planet, in order to "recreate European life on the colonial periphery" (Clark 2003: 163). Colonialism in Australia and New Zealand came at the tail end of this history of attempts at making new Europes around the globe. "It has been said of the New Zealand context, and it is equally true of Australia, that the aim of the colonists was to 'carry with them everything of England but the soil and the climate'" (Clark 2003: 171).

Through processes of naming, Australia was to become, categorically, the container for the European Geographical Unconscious. Australia-as-place quite literally came to be written, through language and histories of inscription across the continent through colonial management and exploration, as the geographical unconscious. However, though Australia is a location – literal, metaphoric, figurative, contemplative – and thus a location wherein the geographical unconscious can reside, it is also only a surface indication of a deeper displacement or disconnect between human and place that lives in the geographical unconscious on the European continent. In other words, in so many ways, Australia was the "other" where Europeans could conveniently re-locate their own anxieties about place and nation.

The subsequent history of exploration of Australia can be seen in terms of a seeking of a particular type of resource extraction that was thwarted:

> Whereas the founding fathers of America believed that they had
> been given a continent in which to build the new Jerusalem, the
> Europeans who came to Australia acknowledged no such manifest
> destiny. On the contrary, the most characteristic response, even of
> those who were not convicts, was a sense of alienation and exile.
> (Haynes 1998: 23)

Despite the fact that explorers of the Central Desert, most notably John MacDouall Stuart, who is responsible for finally mapping the path from South Australia to Darwin, manipulated the reality of the Australian desert landscape in order to fit the British government's need to forge settlement in an ecologically impossible site, the very ecology of the desert landscape waged war against attempts at European containment.

This same desert ecology has come to signify, in the contemporary Australian consciousness, a spiritual center. Roslyn Haynes, in her major survey of the literature, art and film of the Centre and its role in the revaluing of Australian desert space writes that:

> In Australia it is the desert that epitomises this 'before-us' quality.
> In our collective imagination the site of ancient myth, of spiritual
> dimension and cultural rebirth is peculiarly the desert, a landscape
> that for more centuries than European civilization can lay claim to
> has symbolized the land's endurance, provoking creative reap-
> praisals of our place in Nature and the meaning of our existence.
> When we read of progressively older geological and archeological
> finds setting the age of the continent at more than 800 million
> years, the River Finke in Central Australia at 350 million years,
> and Aboriginal habitation nudging 50, 000 years we are scarcely
> surprised. (Haynes 1998: 1-2)

The "hideous blank" that had characterized the British perception of the vast majority of the Australian continent during settlement, that same vast unknown that drove the pathological "imperatives for discovery" (Haynes 1998: 36) that would ultimately bring MacDouall Stuart and many others to an early grave, would come to draw in its own people and call for a radical renegotiation of habitation in this place. Haynes argues that the shift in popular perception of the Australian desert was due largely to the development of "adventure tourism" and a culture of "evangelists for tourism" in the 1940's and 50's that was made possible through the opening up of wilderness spaces in the desert through photographic and four wheel drive technologies.

As artists were able to access otherwise inaccessible locations in airplanes and four wheel drive vehicles and then subsequently apprehend place through painting and photographs to return to the urban centers with documentation of these places, a whole culture of tourism was born. As Australians were able to see the desert depicted in comprehensible terms, interest in the burgeoning industry of adventure tourism was brought forward, marketing particular forms of wilderness experience. Through a limited engagement with the sublime, afforded by technologies of transportation, tourists were able to access and apprehend these wilderness spaces as acts of, at once, adventure and anti-materialism. However, this marked "transformation" in the perception of these places has come at a cost, both in public and social ways and on intellectual terms, as the desert is still inscribed with a sense of "otherness" that it has acquired by virtue of its ability to provide forms of contained experiences of the "wild", geographical and psychological. For Roslynn Haynes, "[i]t is the artists, writers and photographers of the last hundred years who have taught us to see the desert differently" (1998: xii-xiii).

Romantic Anxieties

It seems to me that de Quincey's claim that her training operates at the "sub-cultural" level and McAuley's claim that the training works at the "ontological" level, while very useful framing devices in many respects, do not encompass the full scope of Triple Alice as a site-specific intervention about *place*. De Quincey's "sub-cultural" assertion and McAuley's "ontological" assertion are predicated on an idea of a "before" state, a "prior" state from which BodyWeather and Triple Alice transport participants. In Harrison's account of her experience over the course of the three labs, she expressed that she knew she had arrived at a state of increased intimacy with the desert by articulating her former "shock". She articulated her increased "responsibility" towards the environment by explaining her former "blindness" towards that same place. A "disruption" of the previous state, facilitated by the Triple Alice experience, constituted a modification of former ways of being and thinking.

When Gay McAuley explains that *a profound shift in ontological awareness is what is required if we are to confront the human and ecological legacies of our colonial past*, I think that she could just as easily be invoking a need for what literary scholar Timothy Morton would call "dark ecology" (2007: 181-197). Dark ecology is a radical proposition that calls for an interrogation of the presence of ideas of "nature" within various forms of contemporary cultural practice. Morton contends that *ideas* of nature get in the way of making any real progress in addressing a solution to various *real* environmental crises. Writes Morton, "[s]trange as it may sound, the idea of nature is getting in the way of properly ecological forms of culture, philosophy, politics, and art" (2007: 1). Morton writes from within his expertise of the literature of the Romantic period to reveal the presence of a series of confining and reifying constructs in the form of poetic devices that continue to influence contemporary thought and practice. The "beautiful soul syndrome", for instance, enables one to wash "his or her hands of the corrupt world, refusing to admit how in this very abstemiousness and distaste he or she participates in the creation of that world" (2007: 13). Morton describes a contemporary "ecological imaginary" that is composed of such conflicts. With the phrase "ecological imaginary", Morton is invoking the systems of flow and exchange articulated by Arjun Appadurai in *Modernity at Large* (1995), while still reliant on the Lacanian construction of the concept of the imaginary (1997).

McAuley further punctuates the overall significance of Tess' work in Triple Alice when she writes:

> Changing the way people think and feel about place, providing even a few people with a deeply felt, embodied experience of the complex interconnections between a specific place, its flora and fauna and its human inhabitants may have a more profound impact in the longer term than many more overtly political acts. If the practice of Body Weather affects our way of seeing, doing, understanding and being in place, then it clearly has important political and cultural implications for us at this stage of our national history as we begin to learn to live *with* the land rather than merely taking from it what it can produce or supply, learn what it can give if approached differently, what we need to give in return, and being at last to heed the lessons we can learn from the Indigenous inhabitants of this place. (McAuley 2003: xi)

McAuley's writing suggests that there is a great deal of benevolence towards Tess' BodyWeather process and an enduring articulation of a trust in its powers (even if and when those powers are beyond the powers of articulation). However, not all participants are entirely satisfied to let it rest at "ontology" or "ontology with possible social and political benefits". Maxwell, for instance, is somewhat anxious about his own reception of the experience:

> I have read my own claims for what such a project might achieve,
> or the kinds of questions that might be put to it, as being frankly,
> and, again, unreconstructedly, *Romantic* in aspiration, already
> having fallen into the default of the colonialist gaze. (Maxwell
> 2003: 71)

And so the pendulum swings not only back and forth between sites, between city and desert, between fast and slow, from body to body. The pendulum also swings from microscopic to macroscopic lens, from the personal to the political, from the ontological to the ethical. However, at least in the written documentation that has emerged from the Triple Alice projects, while the authors might initially express aspects of tension or anxiety in the *reception of their reception* of the process, there is a trend toward conclusions that express a resolution of these tensions and anxieties. Maxwell makes this journey in the following way:

> At the heart of my anxiety, then, is a wondering about the claims
> that might be made for a practice such as Body Weather, and for
> work such as the extended TripleAlice project. More specifically,
> I suppose, I am interrogating my own terms of engagement with,
> expectations of, and desires for, such projects: my desire to drag
> them into a socio-political realm, when really, really, the work is
> about the work itself: about possibilities for being and becoming
> at a radically a-cultural level, a level at which the social and the
> political are pushed back beyond the horizon of a pure immersion
> in the flesh of the world, experienced in and through the renegoti-
> ated limits of the flesh of mere bodies. (Maxwell 2003: 71)

While Maxwell, over the course of his article, genuinely wrestles with aspects of what the practice means and what the practice does, he feels the need to come back to an emphatic repetition of the value of the work when he writes *really, really, the work is about the work itself.* Perhaps as much as "Triple Alice is about itself", the writing about Triple Alice is about the writing about Triple Alice.

These challenges in writing about the Triple Alice experience can also be at least partially accounted for in a discussion of ethnography. McAuley describes Tess' own descriptive language as "densely worded" and explains the trend toward lyrical prose in the writings that have emerged out of the Triple Alice experience in the following way:

> It seems that the experience of the Centre and of the TripleAlice project was so powerful that the attempt to account for it somehow exceeds the parameters of normal scholarly prose…The resort to what Ian Maxwell calls his own "somewhat impressionistic prose" is doubtless due in part to the overwhelming physical impact of that desert country, but it is also a result of what Sarah Dunn calls the "de-programming, re-programming process" of Body Weather, which opened up new ways of seeing and experiencing place, and created new levels of sensitivity in all participants, even those on the fringe of the intensive work. (McAuley 2003: x)

Perhaps in this way, the experience, as McAuley describes it, reveals the extent to which all experience "exceeds the parameters of normal scholarly prose", posing yet another ontological question that brings to mind the writing of Sally Ann Ness regarding her own frustrations with ethnographic documentation. Ness discusses the fragmentary quality of ethnography, the partial poetry of the record keeping of systems inherited and invented when she writes:

> These note entries seek to ensure the visibility of their own unfoldings and foreclosures, reflecting the further possibilities for interpretation and invention still available in subsequent site-specific compositions. The gaps in between the dates of writing make openings – voids that are not apertures but closures to the flow of information, closures of the writer's presence, announcing the limits of the view, the turnings of the gaze. They make the steps of composition clearer as well as the no-man's land between the steps. They make the ruptures in the ethnographic process literary realities. (1996: 144)

Perhaps another part of the reason why it is so challenging for Triple Alice participants to communicate their experience in written form has to do with philosopher of place George Seddon's observation that "[l]anguage carries the riches and the burdens of the past, and the language of landscape, like all language, is loaded" (1997: 5). The riches and the burdens of the past, as they live in language and landscape, render conventional prose inadequate for the task of describing the BodyWeather and Triple Alice experience. Participants, seeking an embodied language of place – or a language to match their experience of embodiment-in-place – find themselves collapsing an otherwise "detached" or "all-knowing" subjectivity into the text, thereby "deforming" conventions of literature and creating a hybrid form of writing that exists between percept and philosophy (Muecke 2010: 108-9).

McAuley tries to explain that, in Tess de Quincey's own writing, "language seems under such pressure from the intensity of her memories that prose gives way to a kind of poetry" (McAuley 2003: x). In this sense, de Quincey's desert landscape is, as theorist Simon Schama has recognized, a work of the mind, "built up as much from strata of memory as from layers of rock" (1995: 7). Certain philosophers of place cannot accept such an individualized rendering of place. J. Nicholas Entrikin claims that "we are always 'in place', much as we are always 'in culture'" (1991: 1). For Entrikin, we cannot escape aspects of place as we cannot escape culture. Robert David Sack, however, would be satisfied with Tess' rendering of place, as he has outlined a concept of "place/self", which is constructed through a set of three intersecting spheres that represent "meaning", "nature", and "social relations" (1997). In this model, Sack locates "place/self" at the nexus of these three spheres, demonstrating how humans come to understand identity and agency in the context of experiences of and interactions with place. This focus on individual human actions and outcomes is more in keeping with the logic of BodyWeather training in the Triple Alice context, where individuals may work together in a group, but are always wrestling with experiences and meaning in a very personal, individualized way.

Returning to Tess' remarks at the Practice Research Forum in Sydney in 2006, we can identify yet a final kind of transposition at work:

I thought Australia,
I thought,
yes,
Lake Mungo and then to the Centre!
I was dying to go to the Centre.
And of course,
10 years later I get to Alice for the first time.
And then comes the fascination:
What is this continent?

Tess' logic of place is a site to site (to site ...) logic that is designed to work *across* place. Her thinking starts with "Australia", then goes to the specific site of "Lake Mungo" and then back out to the regional descriptor "Centre". From the Centre, her thinking then travels back out to consider the expanse of "the continent". In other words, from the "whole" of the country (articulated here using the national/geo-political descriptor of Austrlia), Tess then thought of "Lake Mungo" – a very specific landscape within Australia. From her workshops undertaken at Mungo, she was then attracted, drawn, to another specific site, the "Centre", where she carried out Triple Alice 1, 2 and 3 and then *Dictionary of Atmospheres* in 2005. Subsequent to the work in an around Alice – the centre of the Centre – Tess' thinking drew her back out to larger questions related to the Australian continent as a whole. It is as if thinking specifically within a particular site does not hold her to that site. While some of her works are longer-term in their site-specificity – most notably, TA1-3, which led to *Dictionary of Atmospheres* – and while she is not careless in her movements and thinking from site to site, neither is she tethered to a particular location. She seems to go where the creative impulse takes her, with trust in the BodyWeather methodology to establish the integrity of her pursuits. This is not to suggest that her journey is in any way impulsive. Rather, it is to say that de Quincey seems to be drawn to particular sites, which she mines for creative resources; but then she may be drawn to extend or develop the work that she extracted from her relationship with one site in the context of a new site. To this extent, de Quincey's work illuminates the way in which "the more directly the site is pressed toward, the more elusive and complex the point of definition proves to be" (Kaye 2000: 215). In this way, as de Quincey and her collaborators press toward one site, they are, inevitably, pushed toward the elusiveness and complexity of multiple points of definition. The discoveries made at Hamilton Downs in TA 1-3, then, are specific to Hamilton Down but, in Tess' reckoning, are fair game to be staged in Alice Springs, some 100km away, or even at the Sydney Opera House. It is not that one point is equivalent to another, but rather that, through her intensive, pendulous process, one point cannot help but speak to another point. In this sense, place-based knowledge acquisition for de Quincey can be understood as a journey from site to site, fixed temporally but fluid relationally. As Fiona Wilke writes, "[m]emory emerges from these examples as a performative construct, embedded in landscapes and yet fruitfully modified and renegotiated through a range of present relationships to these landscapes" (2007: 41). Within de Quincey's system, there is substantial trust placed in the archive – the journal note, the dry-erase board, the photograph, the audio clip, and the embodied perception – as well as in the act of archiving – even in all of its ambiguities and imperfections. In this mode of performance making, the "truth", or at least the potency of any particular experience, sufficiently archived, will resonate, will vibrate, even if relocated in a new body, in a new site, in a new context.

Landing in Alice: From the Nation to the Centre, Back to Sydney, Back to the Centre … Sydney … Centre, Sydney, Alice

\The Department of Performance Studies, during the month of July in 2005, was a bit like an elaborate family reunion, where memories and documents and archives were floating freely and joyfully and where ever more snapshots were taken, ever more new memories made. The "rift" that Diana Taylor articulates as being "between the *archive* of supposedly enduring materials (i.e., texts, documents, buildings, bones) and the so-called ephemeral *repertoire* of embodied practice/knowledge (i.e., spoken language, dance, sports, ritual)" (2003: 19) – this rift does not exist in this environment. Tess' archival language, her archival systems, her archival processes are not only touching on many sites of memory, but are actively generating an environment of remembering, which Pierre Nora refers to as "milieux de memoire" (1989: 7).

Tess refers to this process of remembering as "keeping the place alive", and uses the phrase especially when trying to communicate how the dancers are meant to retrieve embodied memories. In rehearsals for *Dictionary of Atmospheres* at the University of Sydney, this became especially important as Tess tried to integrate new Company member Tom Davies, who had never been to the Australian desert, and who had only worked on one unrelated Company project in the months just prior.

In the last week of studio rehearsals in the Rex Cramphorn studio, Tess worked for one day just with Peter – the senior Company member – and Tom. This rehearsal was emblematic of the type of translation that Tess tries to affect. One morning was spent in dialogue about several texts that the three had read – works from Pamela Croft and desert anthropologist T.G.H. Strehlow (1961), and Kim Mahood's *Craft for a Dry Lake* (2000). The texts had been selected because of their popularity for participants in the Triple Alice project. Mahood attended TA 3. Strehlow, as the most famous Central Desert anthropologist, has had a significant impact on the Australian understanding of Aboriginal cultural practices. Thus, on that morning, the three – Peter, Tom and Tess – were re-engaging with these texts as a way of reconnecting with some of the core ideas and concepts that had fueled the creative work of Triple Alice. Here again, transposition was taking place in multiple streams. Tess and Peter had been a part of the Triple Alice project from its inception. Tom, on the other hand, was brand new to the Company had had no previous connection to or knowledge of Triple Alice and, further, had never been to the Central Desert at all. Much of this session was about a second kind of transposition, in which Peter, as the eldest Company member and the member with the longest relationship to the Triple Alice project, was transposing his memories of Hamilton Downs and the objectives of the residencies in the desert to Tom, the youngest and least experienced Company member.

In the afternoon, Peter and Tom created choreography with Tess that responded to the language of the texts that they had discussed. Tom had developed a quirky leaping movement that Tess named a "lollop," and she explained to Tom what she saw him doing:

these lollops
(there is a) tendency in your body to be quite tight
(you're) not carrying any baggage
which means you're on top of your weight
(a) slight tension
because you're ready
(there needs to be a) relaxedness about (the) relationship
in the lollop – (the) weight of the lollop

(in Japan, dancing with Min Tanaka and Mai Juku)
(we were) 5 foreigners
(and there was a) review
(")solos by foreigners("):
when (they) first come
(their) bodies (are) like a white page
they glitter so much
after a few years
(there is a)
heaviness
darkness
obscurity
weight
and a softness
outside
inside – learnt from inside
(this is the) opposite of western dance tradition – everything lightness and white
dancing a white page

(it is) another level of availability
sort of into your own body and place
instead of always forwards
that's where we culturally belong
on the white page

(like how) mainstream people walk
a hundred years ago people walked differently
walking the scars of their lives
wonky walks
in Brisbane
after a couple years
all the wonkiness (was) gone

there's nothing there
nothing but consumerization
not a moment

any of those blues people
carry their history with them
(there is a) level of release into the body
for that to become playable
(it is) extremely hard to stand from emptiness
and start from emptiness
(you're) terrified the stuff won't come up

in Danish
(the) word for develop
is to unwind
(it is an) unwinding of your own consciousness
from the inside
(that's) locked into genetics history environment
experiences encoded in the body
having access to them

patterns of return
(are a) European tradition
nomads move
according to season you move different places
but actually retrack your steps
(you) go back to (the) same places
(I'm) not sure about Ab(original) tradition(s)

One of the interesting aspects of Tess' speech here is that she is directing it towards Tom as a way of informing him about the qualities of movement that she values most as a practitioner and she is traveling from site to site to do so. To communicate her values as a choreographer, she uses a site-specific transpositional logic that moves from Tom's body in the rehearsal room to foreign bodies in Japan to bodies that have been in Japan for a few years to bodies of people from 100 years ago to the bodies of "those blues people" to Danish bodies to European nomadic bodies to Aboriginal traditional bodies. She moves through space and time in order to provide Tom with not so much a narrative as a map – a way to imagine his body moving through space and time, "developing" as a process of "unwinding" towards ideas of bodies in other spaces and other times.

"Keeping the place alive" in this context – in the studio with Peter and Tom – expresses that way in which Tess' transpositional logic engages with the specificity of particular sites (even imagined sites) while readily moving between sites to create relationships between forms. Tess does not push for a circumscription of these sites into a camp of sameness. Rather, in her task of training a new Company member, she is compelled to used multiple sites, multiple locations to flesh out what she means: to evoke in Tom's consciousness, in his muscles and bones, the affective qualities that she wishes to see him access as a dancer. In this narrative, if the "blues person" could stand in for the whole, Tess would only use the "blues person" example. If the story about foreign bodies in Japan could serve the purpose, she would only use that story. But Tess needs to draw on all of the examples, all of the sites in order to illustrate a quality of movement that she wants to see in Tom.

Part of the reason for the use of multiple sites is that, ultimately, Tess wants Tom to find his own way of "keeping the place alive" – a means by which his own body can engage in these inherited forms. In another example of transposition, the whole Company was rehearsing a series of "invitations" that had been generated during Triple Alice. Again with Tom, Tess had to reiterate that with these "invitations" – these choreographic snapshots of material created during TA1-3 – the intent was not for Tom to simply copy or replicate what he was seeing the other dancers' do. Rather, Tom needed to derive some sense of the energetic spirit of the movement, the logic, the rationale, the empathetic quality of the gesture, and then take that intelligence into his own body and keep it alive there on his own terms.

'Working Up an Environment': Transposition and the Spinifex Affinity

Tess: What have we done?
Where are we going?
How do we safeguard?
How do you keep the stuff alive in you?
We need to have it cooking very closely to the
surface
We're working
much much more architecturally
clearing architecturally
lines of architecture in the riverbed
We probably need a series of photocopies
to decide this is where we're framing stuff
That conversation needs to be very clearly
mapped out.

Russell: We do spend a lot of time talking, don't we?

Once we arrived in Alice Springs as a collective, there was a whole new set of transposing to be carried out. We had to install equipment and material in the kilometer of riverbed space that we would use. The dancers had to acquaint themselves with this new space and carefully carve out a series of new relationships with the physical geography of the place, using the preexisting choreography to mediate these new relationships. As the Company sought to recapture experiences in the process of interpreting choreography sometimes two months old, sometimes five years old, members as individuals and also as a group came to create a living memorial topography in the environment. The topographic map that they generated was born of a dialogue between their own body maps and the series of spreadsheets that delineated each improvisation, each movement phrase, and described those movements in imaginative detail with a language that the Company had painstakingly developed to help their bodies remember. For Tom, it was a matter of remembering rehearsals in Sydney. For Peter is was remembering back through Sydney and then further to Hamilton Downs 2001, 2000 and 1999.

In *Dictionary of Atmospheres*, materials exploration involved both objects imported into the desert (e.g. large screens for projected video imagery culled over years of filming on- and off-site; several large barrels with televisions sitting in the base, projecting films made by Francesca da Rimini; 200 meters of anti-bird netting; 100 flares aka "tiki torches"; and so on) as well as materials on-site that had fostered choreographic response over the years. One such on-site material of significance to the process was spinifex, a tumbleweed-like grass endemic to the Australian continent and whose (mis)appellation, itself, reflects the application of a external sensibility on the desert environment.

Engagement with spinifex represents the extent to which Tess' creative process involves, as she describes it, "working up an environment". When Tess uses the phrase "working up an environment", she is referring to the circumstance of initially finding herself in Australia without any known collaborators, and how that produced for her an "in-betweenness" that informs the way she makes performances:

> In coming to Australia, because I didn't have a body of people that I worked with who were trained in the same ways I was, I found myself trying to work up an environment and create that training for other people. This in-betweenness is something that I'm constantly folding in and out of. I think that works to the method by which I create performances but also the stages of the work. ('RealTime').

Tess worked to train performers over the years – in some part, through her work with the University of Sydney – and came to find musicians, writers and media artists with whom she could work. In understanding the ways in which she used the plant spinifex in *Dictionary of Atmospheres*, it is useful to reference Tess' notion of "working up an environment", as her engagement with the plant is, in some part, reflective of larger patterns and themes in the ways that she uses materials – including performing bodies. In order to fully articulate the way that the entire Company became involved in the harvesting, sculpting and burning of spinifex in performance, I will need, in the next several pages, to describe some of the practices undertaken with spinifex.

The Curious Life of Spinifex

The harvesting, sculpting and performing of spinifex in the *Dictionary of Atmospheres* process was treasured. Though we had at least five different ways of spelling it in emails exchanged between us, and though the term "spinifex" is not even the appropriate botanical term[11], as spinifex actually is the name of a related coastal grass, participating in the process of traveling to a remote location outside of Alice Springs to dig up the plant in bundles, stuff it in the back of Vic the production manager's ute[12], getting filthy and unreasonably scratched up in the process, and then sending it back to the performance site to be sculpted and prepared for the performance: these harvesting events drew lively participation from performers, production team and even volunteers who had attached themselves to the company. Spinifex Triodia, the actual organic material that we were working with, is an endemic species of grass that covers 25 percent of the continent and at least 50 percent of the desert and has ritual significance for Indigenous groups in Australia. While the company did not concern themselves with understanding the nuanced significance of the grass, they endeavored to create their own ritual around the spinifex which included the harvesting process, followed by the transformation of the spinifex into sculptural bundles, their installation in the performance space of the dry riverbed, the *pas de deux* choreography, and the bonfire at the end.

The most significant trip gather spinifex was the last, in which all five of the Company dancers and almost all of the members of the production team were in attendance. In addition to the task of collecting spinifex that afternoon, we had also budgeted time to conduct the Company's BodyWeather training in a new outdoor space – our first opportunity this trip to train outside the concrete block structure of the Watch This Space arts venue in downtown Alice Springs, which had been our home for a couple of hours of BodyWeather training each morning until now.

In training myself in this new outdoor space – the first time I had trained outdoors with the Company, placed between the red sand at my bare feet and the big skies stretched out above my unadorned head, adjacent to this derelict set of buildings created for a film that was never made, I got the sensation that I was, at last, *really* doing the training. The intense presence of the sun, the risk of a rogue rock interrupting one of my steps, the experience of my

---

[11] Spinifex may refer to: *Spinifex*, a species of grass that grows in coastal areas of Australia. (True Spinifex; Coastal Spinifex) –or– *Spinifex Triodia*, a hummock grass of arid Australia, covering twenty per cent of the Australian continent. Although not technically Spinifex, *Spinifex Triodia* it is commonly referred to as such.

[12] "Ute" is a term used in Australia to refer to a utility vehicle. These vehicles are not as large as "sport utility vehicles" and are more like a hybrid between a car and a small truck.

own linearities defined in the context of the natural desert environment as opposed to an indoor studio space: all of these elements produced and reproduced a sense that I had *arrived* in the Central Desert.

While many of us trained, other members of the group explored the site, on which several structures had been built in anticipation of a film shoot whose budget had subsequently fallen through. Vic, our production manager, walked into the "hotel" structure to find a working piano that he played. Penny, the massage therapist, discovered a dune behind which she played her trumpet. Sam, one of the media artists on the project, documented the site and our activities on video. The Company's photographer, Mayu, and her camera collected images of all of us in the space, turning the experience of place into texts and memories and documents.

Subsequent to the training on the film set, the collection of the spinifex began. What had started out as a chore assigned to the production crew had turned into a whole-group effort – to "harvest" spinifex at this remote location and then prepare bundles of the plant for a series of site-based performances that would take place in the dry riverbed in Alice for the Desert Festival. Company members gathered masses of spinifex with shovels and arms, masses that were then stuffed in the back of Vic's ute – a ute-full of spinifex that we would haul back to our storage space at the Totem Theatre next to the Todd-Mparntwe riverbed.

As we transposed the Company's salient encounters with various sites in this country, we attempted to integrate ourselves into this place through an inexplicable attraction to the material details of the environment. Much of the early work in our experience of site had involved walking through the riverbed and visiting adjacent sites – out to the Hamilton Downs campground where the Triple Alice projects took place; journey to the top of the hillside adjacent to the riverbed, climbing from boulder to boulder at mid-day; traversing the sand as a mob at dusk – and making an attempt to be in place. Tess designed a ritual of having tea in the riverbed, complete with aluminum thermoses and cups for chai that the Company prepared each morning. "What time is it?" is an ongoing, shared joke between Company members, referencing a desire to abandon perceived Western conventions associated with time and temporality and adopt a perceived Aboriginal sensibility of timelessness.

The spinifex masses were subsequently unloaded from Vic's ute and transformed into sculptural bundles. The impetus for the gathering, sculpting, and burning was derived from the multiple histories of transposition that brought the Company members and their creative work into the dry riverbed space. Choreography that had most recently been developed and honed in the Rex Cramphorn studio at the University of Sydney was danced (back) into the sands of the dry Todd-Mpantwe Riverbed. Danced (back) into the sands because it was here, in Alice (sort of, adjacent to), that the choreographic concepts first came into being, over a period of residencies and site visits and imaginings carried out at Hamilton Downs. Documentary film footage and narrative ephemera from Triple Alice reveals a pattern of participants sitting around a fire at the close of a day – a gathering that facilitates the sharing of information collected.

Thus, the spinifex process – the gathering, the sculpting, the dancing with and the use of the bundles as a gathering point, as a "burning point" – referenced and reflected those larger processes of gathering and sharing that members of the Company and others had undertaken in the Triple Alice projects. The curiosity with the spinifex, and particularly the importing of spinifex from a remote location well outside of Alice, is emblematic of the transpositional qualities at work in the Company's creative process. The Company's performance with spinifex reflects how their negotiation of the desert ecology is reflective of their own imported systems of containment: the very notion of harvesting from one site and planting at another, of making the spinifex into something both manageable and beautiful, and the ritual connection in the choreography and then the burning. It also illustrates how the Company's gesture towards "creating a new cultural practice" performs the in-between space, the poetic meeting grounds of the colonial legacies of containment and the history of ecological resistance to that containment.

Wild Things

> Amidst all the forms of disorder and 'deterritorialization' accompanying colonization, biological forces stand out as the most irruptive and unpredictable – and the least amenable to re-containment.
>
> – Nigel Clark (2003: 163)

Just before Ian Maxwell begins his wrestling match with the meaning of Triple Alice 1, he writes the following passage:

> Extraordinary things … extraordinary ways of seeing people, of experiencing being. Tess and her crew, hyped up on isolation,

> physical beauty, exhaustion, macrobiotic food, distance, loneliness. (Maxwell 2003: 70)

This is the kind of lyrical prose that Gay McAuley explains is common among participants who try to capture the Triple Alice experience. McAuley has accounted for this by positing that the desert environment, itself, is profound, and that the experience of the desert, in many respects, is beyond words, beyond explanation. This passage from Maxwell appears after 2000 lyrical words, after which he pauses and writes "And yet..." (2003: 70). What follows "and yet" is the previously quoted passage, in which Maxwell struggles to determine whether his response to the desert, in the context of Triple Alice, is really just *Romantic*, and he expresses some concern about that possibility. Why would this be a concern for Maxwell? Because he is afraid that perhaps he has "already fallen into the default of the colonialist gaze" (Maxwell 2003: 71).

The latent history that informs the De Quincey Company's "creation of a new cultural practice" through its spinifex ritual tells us that, invariably, certain aspects of that history will emerge when the "new cultural practice" is brought forward and shared with an unindoctrinated public. The Triple Alice art labs were private, cloistered spaces with attendant logics and languages that were, as Maxwell writes, inevitably "blinkered" (2003: 71). This seems paradoxical at first, as the BodyWeather practice is concerned with receiving, interpreting and expressing the experience of *place* writ large, but attention to the actual doing of the art-labs reveals that the practice cultivates a focus on micro-topographies. However, this is not so much a matter of a paradox, as it is a matter of limited public exposure. Hamilton Downs and the Rex Cramphorn Studio served as "wombs" for the creation of the desired new cultural practice. Perhaps it is not so surprising that, when the De Quincey Company birthed its infant cultural practice on the hostile grounds of the Todd-Mpartnwe riverbed, under the tripled public gaze of a small regional community arts festival, audiences did not understand – or, were unable to participate fully.

Roslynn Haynes explains that, on a national level, "it is the artists, writers and photographers of the last hundred years who have taught us how to see the desert differently" (1998: xiii). Of the many examples that Haynes draws upon in her book, *Seeking the Centre*, it is perhaps her discussion of Robyn Davidson's *Tracks* (1980) that resonates most strongly with the work of de Quincey. In 1977, as a beautiful, mysterious and young white woman, Davidson made an epic 1,700-mile solo journey from Alice Springs across the Western Desert to the Indian Ocean with four camels and a dog, purportedly to escape the "boredom" of her city life in Brisbane and the "self-indulgent negativity" of her generation (Wyndham 2007). Her memoir, *Tracks*, which made her an international sensation, catapulted Davidson into the media spotlight as the "Camel Lady". Haynes contextualizes Davidson's journey when she writes:

> The wealth and materialism of the 1980s in Australia generated a general if vague desire for something more spiritually and psy-chologically satisfying than the ease and luxury that money could provide. In a secular approximation to monastic regimen, physical hardships, voluntarily undertaken and combined with solitude, were popularly regarded as the path to psychological self-discovery. Travel to the outback was believed to offer life-changing potential by realigning priorities. (1998: 270).

Davidson's was the "first extended autobiographical account of such a pilgrimage" (Haynes 1998: 270) and, as such, it spoke to a generation of Australian readers, while also invariably referencing the desert explorations of the nineteenth-century. Haynes explains that the book:

> presents the closest feminine counterpart of the nineteenth-century explorers' engagement with the Australian desert, provid-ing a perspective that was almost wholly absent from reports of expeditions to the Centre. (1998: 271)

The work simultaneously exists very much as a product of its own time:

> Although retaining the asceticism associated with the biblical so-journ in the 'wilderness', Davidson, unlike the nineteenth-century explorers, makes no pretence of altruism. Indeed, she is less interested in the desert as such, or even as an ecological location, than in coming to terms with it as personal space. (Haynes 1998: 271)

In this regard, Davidson's journey and memoir emerge from "a sense of inner compulsion about the need to undertake this task rather than a concern for externally generated goals" (Haynes 1998: 271). Haynes creates a list of the values implicit in Davidson's trek, such as:

> the importance of colours rather than the economic potential and functional deployment of the land; the sense of solitude and material privation as a prerequisite for self-knowledge; the traditional trope of the journey as initiation into enlightenment; and most, significantly, the emphasis on the dream as the immediate path to understanding and Truth. Davidson also stresses the irrational and non-quantifiable aspects of discovery. (Haynes 1998: 271).

The list relies on a set of oppositions – colors of the land take priority over the economic potential of the land, discovery is posited as irrational and non-quantifiable rather than material and functional. Within these oppositions, Haynes notes the way in which the values expressed by Davidson exist simultaneously as traditional and contemporary. Haynes' list also illustrates how the goals of Davidson's journey live in implicit opposition to some of the ideological frameworks that undergirded the work of nineteenth-century explorers – ideological frameworks that continued to exert an influence in 1980, and are arguably still at work today.

This approach to her experience, processed through her memoir, has a profound personal affect on Davidson, who transforms from a "disgruntled, impractical, resentful outsider, quick to anger and fear" into a "desocialised wild woman who walks naked through the desert" (Wyndham 2007). Reflecting on *Tracks* twenty-seven years after its publication, Susan Wyndham echoes Haynes' observation that the work emphasizes self-discovery, personal space, inner compulsion and self-knowledge, when she writes that Davidson "loses herself as a white, urban woman and becomes much closer to the Pitjantjara[13] people ... and learns their way of relating to the land." (Wyndham 2007). Davidson writes extensively about the personal, developmental experiences that shape her along the way, articulating her resulting perspective on the self as follows:

> The self does not seem to be an entity living somewhere inside the skull, but a reaction between mind and stimulus ... The self in a desert becomes more like the desert. It has to, to survive. It becomes limitless, with its roots more in the subconscious than the conscious – it gets stripped of non-meaningful habits and becomes more concerned with realities related to survival. (Davidson 1980: 213).

---

[13] Pitjantjara is the name of a group of Aboriginal people who are from the Central Australian Desert.

Although Wyndham "worried" that Davidson "was romanticizing the Aboriginal people out of sympathy and hostility to her own people", she eventually resolves this concern by determining that, ultimately, Davidson's perspective is "sensible" given her circumstances, concluding that "clearly Davidson found her natural state in the desert" (2007).

Though Triple Alice and *Dictionary of Atmospheres* participants were not exposed to the level of isolation, vulnerability and danger that Davidson experienced, there is nonetheless a kinship between the narratives that have emerged from the desert journeys facilitated by Davidson and de Quincey. Participants in de Quincey's desert art-labs and performances, like Davidson, generated within themselves reverence for the desert environment. In their narrative reflections on the experience, they consistently return to intimate analysis of the personally transformative effects of the desert environment, which hinge on the intersection of "losing" and "finding" oneself.

Keeping in mind Haynes' argument that it is the artists, writers and photographers who have taught Australia, as a nation, to "see the desert differently", perhaps an interesting way to think about the function of transposition in the De Quincey process comes from Claude Levi-Strauss. Levi-Strauss, while trying to articulate how *totems* work in the necessarily problematic categories of "high" and "low" art, or, "Western" and "primitive" forms, landed on the notion of "quantitative transposition" (1966 [1962]: 23). Quantitative transposition, he argued, could account for the process whereby an art object is able to communicate an otherwise impossibly "formidable" concept. In some cases, an artist can tackle such a difficult subject and create an object in such a way that a viewer can "apprehend" the otherwise inarticulable. The object, the artistic creation, is the "homologue of the thing" (Levi-Strauss 1966 [1962]: 23) which "constitutes a real experiment with the thing on a metaphorical level" (Reynolds 2004: 139).

The aim of Triple Alice centered around the "pre-" or "a-" cultural: to get *below* culture or *before* culture. In some respects, BodyWeather is designed to train the culture "off" of participants. But the culture – myriad, diffuse, eclectic, elusive – is in them. The culture – divergent, asynchronous, mediated, taxonomic – has produced them. And so the feral – the "wild" element – in this encounter is not where you might think it would be. The feral does not emerge solely in the disobedience of a spinifex plant – its inability to sustain a flame that might hold an audience in the space long enough to punctuate the end-point of a performance. The feral is "haunting" the place, the Triple

Alice practices, and their aftermath, as the artists involved seek to "breathe the land's ghost breath" (Goodall 2006: 120).

The feral is also living in the group's very *desire* to void themselves of culture, as was the desire of Robyn Davidson. The feral is in Sarah Dunn's observation that BodyWeather in Triple Alice is concerned with "drawing us closer to what has long been considered a 'primitive' way of apprehending the world" (2003: 45). The feral is in Dunn's reflections on her personal experience when she reaches towards an understanding of "Aboriginal reality" by way of a reference to Davidson, herself:

> It became more obvious that I existed as part of a whole 'net' or system, that in terms of my sheer 'belonging' to it, my humanness held no more status than an ant's or a tree's. This comprehension perhaps marked a move closer to the edges of how an Aboriginal person apprehends the world. Aboriginal reality, their vision of the world as experienced by Robyn Davidson, is something that they could never be separate from... (2003: 45)

The feral is even in Maxwell's description of the Triple Alice crew as being "hyped up on isolation, physical beauty, exhaustion..." (2003: 70). The feral, here exists not only in the desire to access the pre-cultural or a- or sub-cultural. Nor is the feral solely extant in the articulation of a desire for what the group understands – in a popular sense – to be an Aboriginal reality. The feral then, is that unwieldy set of anxieties that crop up and inform the Company's practices, somewhat against their will, but that, in performance, under the scrutiny of public attention, can announce themselves as candidates for ongoing negotiation.

It is significant, then, when looking through the flames of that final bonfire in *Dictionary of Atmospheres*, to try to *empathize on a cellular level* with the De Quincey Company – to try to understand that the fire was a strategy of communicating a deep love and respect for the desert place, and the impact that it had had on cohorts of participants in the Triple Alice trilogy. It was a very effective tool in the Triple Alice context. It was effective even in the rehearsals just days before the festival performance. It's failure to achieve the kind of spectacular connection between the group and the audience should not simply be indicative of the paradox of the disruption of the desert ecology as an effort to express admiration for and connection to that same ecology. Rather, the Company's offering might be seen as a means by which audiences could witness the unresolved cultural anxieties that few are willing to discuss – because they are afraid they'll get it wrong.

Stretching Time, Writing 'Groundless Forms of Meaning': Inviting an Aporetic Consciousness of Reflection into Performance's Aftermath

Outlining the seven sequential elements that constitute the lifespan of a performance (training, workshops, rehearsals, warm-ups, performance, cool-down, and aftermath), Richard Schechner contends that practitioners "have investigated training, rehearsals and performances but have slighted workshops, warm-up, cool-down and aftermath" (1985: 16). The practitioners that Schechner describes favor those processes that lead directly to the product – in this case, the performance – which, seemingly, has the most value and is the *raison d'être* for all involved. The other neglected elements – workshops, warm-up, cool-down and aftermath – are perceived as ancillary or, perhaps, so excessively idiosyncratic that they do not warrant attention.

Of all of the components of the seven-part sequence, it is aftermath, defined as "the long-term consequences or follow-through of a performance" (Schechner 1985: 19) that receives the least amount of attention. Aftermath, as outlined by Schechner, is a broad temporal category that encompasses such heterogeneous practices as "the changes in status or being that result from an initiatory performance" or "the slow merging of performer with a role he plays for decades" as well as the reviews and criticism, theorization and scholarship that might impact performers and understandings of performance-making over time (1985: 19). Arguably, this last category of activity within aftermath – performance theorization and scholarship – has only proliferated in the decades that have passed since Schechner wrote *Between Theatre and Anthropology* in 1985. However, theorization and scholarship *about* aftermath written from within performance practice – that is, the theorization and scholarship which investigates the long-term consequences and follow-through of a performance written from the perspective of the performance-maker – is sparse.

Certain exceptions exist. Writings by Konstantin Stanislavski, Bertolt Brecht, Jerzy Grotowski, Anne Bogart, and Tim Etchells – which provide extensive discussion of practice *over time* from within each director's experience – constitute only part of the growing canon of literature by directors, in particular. That said, even within and among these familiar sources, a reader is called upon to intuit various shifts in each writer's thinking over time. That is to say, while many of the aforementioned writers have penned reflections and arguments at several *moments* throughout their careers, few of them have examined questions regarding the long-term consequences and follow-through of *particular* performance events and experiences.

This bias toward analysis of the recent, the immediate, and the momentary is prevalent also in the reflective writing from performance-as-research (PaR) scholars. On the one hand, reflective and/or analytical writing about PaR and its aftermath becomes central to the practice, itself (or – the *praxis*, if one is to operate from perspective that action and reflection work dialogically). This, coupled with the pressure to demonstrate art's positive "effects" (Baldacchino 2009; Thompson 2011) has limited the generative possibilities of reflective scholarly writing in the field, in some instances reducing narratives, rhetorically and conceptually, to testimonies of personal and professional growth. Jonothan Neelands, writing about applied theatre research in particular, explains the proclivity among PaR scholars in the field to produce "evangelised reports of personal victories in making miracles happen against all odds" (Neelands 2004: 47). On the other end of the spectrum lives the critique of practice, written from inside a training or performance experience, in which the methods and concepts associated with a particular paradigm are interrogated (see, for instance, Gates 2011; Taylor 2010). Although, in some cases, evangelized reports might serve an important purpose, and critiques are surely welcome and necessary forms of dialogue – the problem I seek to articulate here is not so much regarding particular outcomes, as it is the problematic perception within our field regarding the relationship between practice and writing. In Neelands' "evangelized reports" example, it is the report – *the writing* – which is blamed. And critiques of practice, often rich in detail, steeped in many years of embodied experience, still have the capacity to miss significant aspects of that embodied experience, when translated into a written document. Even within the rich territory of the rethinking of "performance as philosophy" (Cull 2012) and the "difference of performance as research" (Fleishman 2012) a dichotomy between "making" and "writing" continues to be reinforced.

In this epilogue, which serves as the terminus to a piece of writing that has sought to understanding the making of several moments in the work of Tess de Quincey and the De Quincey Company, I would like to propose that the affective turn in performance scholarship, which has elevated the status of PaR in some respects, requires a corresponding re-examination of existing models of reflective practice, which compartmentalize reflection temporally and orient the writer towards reflection as a form of "problem-solving," implicitly encouraging narratives of amelioration. The temporal boundaries of *beginning* and *end*, set up by Dewey in his recommendation that reflection take place "at the beginning, to determine more definitely and precisely the nature of the difficulty to be dealt with" and "at the end, to test the value of some hypothetically entertained conclusion" (Dewey 1910: 77), exact a reductive influence on reflection's potential. Although Schön (1983, 1987), Moon (1999, 2006) and others (Carlile and Jordan 2007; Newman 2000), have relaxed Dewey's temporal framework in order to promote a sense of the "on-goingness" of practice by advocating for processes of reflection-in-action and storytelling-as-reflection, reflective practice frequently remains fixed within a social sciences-based orientation towards instrumental reason, which is predicated on a linear construction of time in which an event is understood to have discrete points of beginning, middle and end. Peter Woods (1993), for instance, suggests that we cannot know that any particular educational experience has been "critical" for our development until it has ended and we reflect on the event. Note in Woods' logic that there is an assumption that an experience has a finite ending point. To this extent, Woods' perspective on reflection – or, a retrospective analysis of one's work and its impact, which is presumed to occur in a time and space perceived to be *other* and *apart from* the time and space of the experience – bears a relationship to the way that others have conceived of reflection as a linear, cumulative and ultimately sequential practice in which the value of experience can only truly be appreciated *after* and *away from* the discrete event of the experience, itself.

Baldacchino (2008, 2009) suggests that arts-based research, released from the confines of social sciences-informed approaches to learning and knowledge production, must be characterized by the *aporia*, paradox, groundlessness and divergent thinking characteristic of the arts, themselves. Baldacchino recommends that we embrace art's "groundless forms of meaning" which are "beyond product and process" (2008: 244). In conversation with Baldacchino's thinking, I would like to link Sally Mackey's (2012) inquiry into how students and teachers remember past arts events. Mackey engaged in a retrospective analysis of a performance event from her distant past – a school play that she directed in the 1990s – which prompted her to revisit the way in which she and her students had archived the event, creating a series of "sites of memory". Mackey's retrospective approach, considered in light of Baldacchino's recommendation that arts-based research seek out paradox and divergence in analysis of practice, has inspired me to uncover the paradoxical and aporetic aspects of my encounter with Tess de Quincey and the De Quincey Company, July – September 2005. Now event from my past – it is an event that occurred many years ago in linear time, but which produces in me a feeling of its ongoingness even as I live in the present, at an increasing distance from the moment upon which I reflect. Accordingly, this epilogue draws on fragments of reflective writing that I've collected, collated and manipulated in response to a performance training experience now eight years old. Seeking out examples from within my archival cache of a hybrid form of performative-reflective composition, I have endeavored to work from Anne Brewster's idea of a writing that "literalizes a post-retrieval idea of memory" in which writing "is not an instrument of the retrieval of stored information" but instead is "characterized as a technology of memory, and memory as *tekhne*, writing" (2005: 397).

To this extent, I will explore these writings as a set of attempts or gestures that seek to include, to incorporate, to absorb reflective writing as a performative act (Langellier 1999; Pelias 1994; Pollock 1998; Spry 2001) and as a generative process (Ness 1996; Phelan 1995) that lives within the "what" and "when" of performance-making, although it occurs *after* the "performance" is over. I am seeking to stretch time, or, rather, to lay down a fabric of writing that stretches over my experience of the pastness of then, while also accommodating my experience of the presentness of then, or, how "then" is "now". This is to say that, because my experience of re-membering or re-animating this training gives rise to a non-linear experience of time, I have come to find a need to create a kind of writing that is also productive of a non-linear experience of time (even as it seeps back into the conventional categorical confines of how I imagine time). Also as part of my time stretch, I am seeking to *wrap time around* Schechner's seven sequential elements, as the following discussion of aftermath will involve discussion of a performance training experience, thereby conjoining "aftermath" as the designated "end" of the performance sequence with "training" as the designated "beginning" of the performance sequence. As a means of offering an image for guidance in how I am conceptualizing (or, feeling) this time-stretch, I would like to invoke Martha Graham in her iconic stretchy-fabric tube of costume from her 1930 work *Lamentation*.

I would like to suggest that Graham's body, for my purposes, exists at the kinetic interstices of writing and memory. The fabric, which contains while also amplifies the extension of Graham's body, is a kind of mediating device, or technology, which might (roughly) be likened to an instrument such as a pen, pencil or typewriter used in the writing act. *These analogies are immediately imperfect for me, even as I write them.* However, the images continue to *do* something for the discussion, even as they limit or perhaps even pervert my argument. In this sense, the performative-reflective writing that I am seeking to create might be understood in the terms that Rebecca Schneider lays out in her discussion of "re-performance":

> Touching time against itself, by bringing time *again and again* out of joint into theatrical, even anamorphic, relief presents the real, the actual, the raw and the true as, precisely, the zigzagging, diagonal, and crookedly imprecise returns of time. (2011: 16)

To this extent, in the narrative example to follow, I am interested in charting the way in which narrative and temporal entropy will continue to exert itself within these exercises, drawing me back into precisely the generic structural chasms and collapse into positive(istic) outcomes that I seek to resist. I ask for the experiment to stretch time – but I will inadvertently collapse time with each act of writing. I ask for the experiment to accommodate incongruity, paradox and aporia, but each act of writing will still potentially account for something concrete, fixing points of meaning against my better intentions.

The Experiment – I, You, She: Becoming Person in Training

How long does it take for a training experience to sink into you?
I mean: really *sink in.*
Is it a slow drip?
Leaky faucet.
>   *Percolating coffee.*
Does it rush forth?

> *A summer thundershower.*
> *A breaking levy.*

At what point do you feel that it has become a part of you?
> *Just before you are ready to operationalize it for a show?*
> *During the execution of something difficult, something   technical?*
> *Just after you've taught it to someone else?*

Or, are you like me? You live and re-live formative training experiences over and over again.

You: growing out your relationship to practice in a series of episodes unbounded by time and space.

You: walking down a city street, minding your own business, surging towards your pedestrian destination, and – spontaneous combustion – you realize something you hadn't before about that training you thought was locked in a rehearsal room from a different lifetime.

When does training begin and end?

Eight years ago I was preparing for a two month trip to Australia, where I would become an intern for Tess de Quincey. De Quincey's technical expertise is in BodyWeather: cultivated over the years that she trained and performed as part of Min Tanaka's company Mai Juku; extended further as she adapted that practice in the development of her own company in Australia.

Eight years ago equals 2005, and in 2005 De Quincey and five of her dancers were in the midst of making a performance called *Dictionary of Atmospheres*. I would begin my journey by meeting them for their rehearsals in Sydney. Four weeks after my arrival, we would travel to Alice Springs, in the Australian Central Desert, where there would be more rehearsing and then setting the piece for performance in a dry riverbed for the Alice Desert Festival.

Being an intern meant that I would take on an assortment of small responsibilities, which were *to be determined* once I arrived. Fix props and make them functional. Distribute publicity. Organize a party in Alice. Once in a while – get coffees. It also meant that I would be able to train with the De Quincey Company while they were in rehearsal in Sydney and Alice.

Now I would get to bring my body into that system – *that system, that system, that unknown to me system* – even if only for a short time.

The anticipated outcomes for me as a performer? Like my intern responsibilities, they also were *to be determined*. I was a university student from California at the time – my relationship to practice was imbricated within that receptive role: to do what the instructor asks, to become what the director wants. I had yet to ask my own questions about how my training might impact me in the long run. I lacked the distance – the separation from the immersion of school – to know how. And perhaps because there was such a sense of that vast unknown from the outset, various dimensions of the two months in Australia have lingered with me ~ substantially ~ for all of these years.

That training is, I think, still sinking in.

In what follows I wish to share an experiment in navigating this multi-dimensional temporal space of training. Asking: what happens to a training experience after it is over, but not done – still being integrated? Eight years and thousands of miles separate me from the points of origin from which my memories depart. And yet I've convinced myself that this experience constitutes what Peter Woods calls a "critical educational event", in that I was not only trained with specific skills, but that the event helped me "become person" (1993: 2). Woods explains that such critical events promote "education and development in uncommonly accelerated ways", leading participants to "make great leaps forward" and "discover new things about the self" (1993: 2).

This sits right with me. I became (another) person over the course of that summer.

So I think.
So I think.

Accordingly, my experimental question is this: how might the *before, during* and *after* of training correspond narratively to an exploration of *grammatical person*? Specifically, what might be produced in matching a *before* memory with the first person ("I"), a *during* memory with the second person ("you"), and an *after* memory with the third person ("she")?

In this experiment, I am attempting to extend Monica Prendergast's (2003) concept of "soliloquizing as reflective practice". Prendergast points out that "soliloquy happens when our acting 'I' engages with our reflective 'Me'" (2003). In my adaptation, rather than clinging to the I/Me over time, I'm proposing that an implicit shift in "person" might take place over the course of a training experience that constitutes a critical educational event. Or, to problematize the very system I've just set up – my reminiscent narrative is superimposing a shift in "person" over top the scattered, fractured atlas images that I've held onto, nurtured, perverted over time. And so: all of this is not to suggest that the (my) "I" actually gets left behind for some (other) "You" and is finally replaced by the (strange) "She" in a move towards increasing objectivity or selflessness. Rather, I am proposing that this shift might occur in spatial terms. I am attempting to project different variable locations of self. Of course, the "I" still lives inside all three narratives (*it is me we are talking about ... yes ... ok ... I know this ...*), but by toying with the various pronouns, I experiment with different valences of self. By describing self as "you", my self takes up a different spatial location in my imagination – and hopefully in yours. By describing self as "she", myself takes up a different spatial location in my imagination – and hopefully yours.

The shift is one of *focus* rather than *identity* per se. When a participant enters a new training experience – one that represents a substantial departure from previous training, in a new context, with new people – there is a bit of that experience of "solitude in public". One is aware of other performers in the space, and perhaps even of a watching audience. But relationships to those *others* and, indeed, to the technique itself, have not been formed. Over time, as the training, the environment, and the others in the room become increasingly familiar, a participant's sphere of focus expands. Like the circles of light that Stanislavski uses to explain how an actor can manage her concentration of attention, "as the circle grows larger, the area of your attention must stretch" (Stanislavski 1989 [1936]: 84).

Let's see what happens when I stretch the grammatical person from I to You and from You to She. Prendergast's soliloquizing "I/Me" remains (in reality) the center of all three narratives. I am, after all, still describing myself. But is there anything to be gained from describing myself-as-other?

***

Before – I

I enter the rehearsal room. The University of Sydney's Rex Cramphorn Studio. Everything goes without saying. Others are on the floor. Crouched down. Right hand side of the room. Buckets filled with water. Wet cloths – dunked into bucket, lifted up, hovering above, wrung out, and – laid out on the floor. Two hands travel the cloth across the floor, sending a line of moisture to the other side of the room. Turn around. Push the wet cloth back across the floor to the point of origin.

I want to be helpful.

But what if I get it wrong. Watching. Intercepting visual details. This all seems important. We're not just washing the floors, the dancers are elongating their bodies in a traveling stretch that sends them across the floor with the cleaning project. I realize already I'm dressed inappropriately. But I think I've seen enough to walk over to the starting position and participate in this activity. And: it begins. I'm moving across the floor in a downward dog-type posture. Keenly aware of belly fat hanging below me. Wondering if I'll make it to the other side of the room without crashing into someone else. Wondering if I'll be asked to: stop. Just – stop – that's alright – we've got it. You can just – sit to the side. But no one comes. No one stops me. And I – well – I don't run into anybody.

During – You

You stand softly, quietly, in a red powder dustbowl.

Everything goes without saying.

Lines are formed, as lines are formed, for the MB (muscle and bone; mind and body) training. You travel across the floor. No, not floor, now. It's ground, earth, dust. Strengthening and stretching. Casting yourself through space. Undeniably aware of the large open sky above you. Endless expanse of blue like a color study against the red orange rust palate below. The omnipresent sun in charge and ... dust, dust, dust.

Kicking up red earth dust.

Mostly individual work at first, as it always is. Soft feet simple traveling right down the line. Then start again at the beginning. Movements become more challenging. More demanding. Walking becomes hopping. Hopping becomes leaping. Awareness of your place in the line. Always. Awareness of the symphony of movement cascading across this space like notes organized on the measured rows of a piece of sheet music.

You are a note on a page.

After – She

Restaging her training in Sacramento.

She has it all set up in the backyard. Backyards are small in downtown Sacramento. Just enough space for one line – her line – she's the only one doing this. Duplex on her left. Apartment complex on her right. Little bit of a fence in between.

Everything goes without saying.

She is: walking across the grass. Walking becomes hopping. Hopping becomes leaping. Awareness of her place in space. No one in the duplex or the apartments would know if she was doing it right or wrong. But she's still asking questions. Living backwards in time. Reaching back towards a set of experiences and observations by hurtling herself forward in this here and now. In the backyard. In Sacramento.

***

How long has it taken for this training experience to sink into me?
I mean: really *sink in.*

At what point did the novice I who first walked into the rehearsal room in Sydney become the only-slightly-more-experienced you of the desert? Is the post-experience she merely a re-enactor of an increasingly distant past?

When does training begin and end?

It strikes me that in rehearsing these stories for you here, now – in restaging these memories by arranging letters on an illuminated screen – I am not in fact becoming one or the other of these people.

I was always me, as I was you, as I was she.

Of course. All three memories could have been written in the first, second or third person.

Perhaps training, in this reflexive space, at this reflective moment, is not a matter of becoming (other). Becoming person in this sense has more to do with an expansion of capacity. A proliferation of characters.

End Note

Efforts to validate performance-as-research have led, in some instances, to an unfortunate misrepresentation of the act of reflective or analytical writing as "oppositional" to the making of performance. Cull wishes to protect performance as an independent, autonomous category of activity, adjusting the implicit assumption that performance is a passive practice to which or on which is applied the logic of "text-based research" (2012: 25). This is an important – an essential – move. However, it complicates the landscape of reflective and analytical writing that emerges out of PaR. Because, as Fleishman indicates, "traditional textual scholarship" (2012: 29) is associated with a "particular technology of communicating" (2012: 30) – that is, *writing* – the potential for a radical performative-reflective writing associated with PaR has been heretofore submerged beneath the primary agenda of establishing independent, autonomous *ground* for performance practice. Accordingly, I would like to suggest that, at this point, PaR is uniquely positioned to absorb (claim) reflective writing not as that which lives, categorically and epistemologically on the 'other side' of performance, but within the generative space of performance, itself. In other words, I propose that performative-reflective writing has, potentially, always already been a part of performance practice and, by extension, performance research. Looking to journals of actors in rehearsal, directors preparing for a show, designers marking on a page – these are all spaces in which such writing has been underway for a very long time. Embracing the radical otherness of this kind of writing and playing with its expository potential (rather than relegating it to a narrow empiricism which relegates it to the status of artifact) could lead to a further reconciliation between practice and research.

In order to do this, however, one must fully contemplate not only the way in which "performance is philosophy" and "performance is different" (which are important assertions), but also the way in which art is *neither* product *nor* process:

> Art is not a product, even when there seems to be an object called *art*. Likewise art cannot be reduced to a process, even when many make an argument for art as a process in order to avoid it becoming a product. To define art from within the paradoxical assumption that it is an *in-between* would help us understand the art form's open character. (Baldacchino 2008: 244)

According to Baldacchino, art as an *in-between* is a reference to art's groundlessness. In the making/doing of art, there is no ground *per se*, but rather a horizon, a set of endless possibilities. The traps associated with articulating the value of art, or, more specifically, the value of performance, include the inadvertent de-valuing of what art *is* and what art *can do*. The divergent methods of art (if we can even say that methods, in the conventional sense, exist), the paradoxical nature of the art experience, and the aporetic consciousness of action and reflection built into the *art act*, when translated, are too easily lost. Writing, itself, which fits so neatly into extant academic and intellectual paradigms, has bedeviled the process of re-valuing art and performance. However, my suggestion is that it is not the act of writing, itself, that is the trouble. Instead, it is the way that we understand the categories and temporalities of performance (in which, for instance, training is somehow apart from performance and performance is somehow apart from aftermath) and the way we have implicitly delimited the potentialities of a performative-reflective writing practice, that have led to chronic dissatisfaction with writing as an instrument in and of PaR. My proposal is that the more that writing emerging out of or as part of PaR embraces the great unknown, unexpected, divergent qualities associated with rehearsal processes, the more that writing will be seen as kin to performance, rather than sitting in judgment apart or away from performance.

As a pair of closing thoughts, I would like to leave you with the idea of Robert Smithson's 1965 work *Enantiomorphic Chambers*, which was recreated in 1999. What is important to understand about the works is that they are "enantiomorphic" sculptures (mirror images of each other which are not identical to each other) composed of painted steel and mirrors. In addition to the dialogue that exists between the two sculptures, themselves, there are the many different dialogues that exist in the reflections and refractions that are played out between the mirrored surfaces. What is produced, in this instance, is a literal manifestation of the "groundlessness" of which Baldacchino writes. Or, in the words of Gaston Bachelard, an "intimate immensity" (1994 [1958]: 183). By virtue of the fact that the mirrored surfaces perform and re-perform with limitless possibilities, they are replete with potential meaning, but meaning which is always shifting and, to some degree, contained within the chambers in which they are housed. Such is the potential for a restoration of performative possibility within the reflective writing on PaR.

Bibliography

'About BodyWeather'. On line at: http://dequinceyco.net/bodyweather/about/ (consulted 07.09.2013).

Allan, Grant E. and Richard I. Southgate. 2002. 'Fire Regimes in the Spinifex Landscapes of Australia', in Bradstock, Ross Andrew, Jann Elizabeth Williams, A.M. Gill (eds), *Flammable Australia: The Fire Regimes and Biodiversity of a Continent*. Cambridge: Cambridge University Press, 2002.

Althusser, Louis. 2005 [1965]. *For Marx* (tr. Ben Brewster). London and New York: Verso.

Appadurai, Arjun. 1995. *Modernity at Large: Cultural Dimensions of Globalization*. Minneapolis and London: University of Minnesota Press.

Bachelard, Gaston. 1994 [1958]. *The Poetics of Space* (tr. Maria Jolas). Boston: Beacon Press.

Bailes, Sarah Jane. 2010. *Performance Theatre and the Poetics of Failure*. London: Routledge.

Baldacchino, John. 2009. 'Opening the Picture: On the Political Responsibility of Arts-based Research: A Review Essay'. *International Journal of Education & the Arts* 10 (3): 1-15.

—. 2008. 'The Praxis of Art's Deschooled Practice'. *JADE* 27 (3): 241-260.

Bataille, Georges. 1989 [1973]. *Theory of Religion* (tr. Robert Hurley). Brooklyn: Zone Books.

Bergmark, Johannes. 1991. *Butoh: Revolt of the Flesh in Japan and a Surrealist Way to Move*. Stockholm: Mannen paa qatan.

Blair, Rhonda. 2008. *The Actor, Image, and Action: Acting and Cognitive Neuroscience*. New York: Routledge.

Blair, Rhonda and John Lutterbie. 2011. 'Introduction: *Journal of Dramatic Theory and Criticism's* Special Section on Cognitive Studies, Theatre, and Performance'. *Journal of Dramatic Theory and Criticism* 25 (2): 63-70.

Bourdieu, Pierre. 1990 [1980]. *The Logic of Practice*. Stanford: Stanford University Press.

Brecht, Bertolt. 1992 [1936]. 'Theatre for Pleasure or Theatre for Instruction', in *Brecht on Theatre: The Development of an Aesthetic* (tr. John Willett). New York: Hill and Wang: 69-76.

Brewster, Anne. 2005. 'The Poetics of Memory'. *Continuum: Journal of Media & Culture Studies* 19(3): 397-402.

Brown, Paul. 2006. 'Maralinga: Theatre from a Place of War', in McAuley, Gay (ed.), *Unstable Ground: Performance and the Politics of Place*. Bruxelles: P.I.E. Peter Lang: 205-226.

Carlile, Orison and Anne Jordan. 2007. 'Reflective Writing: Principles and Practice', in O'Farrell, Ciara (ed.), *Teaching Portfolio Practice in Ireland: A Handbook*. Dublin: Centre for Academic Practice and Student Learning, Trinity College Dublin: 24-38.

Carroll, John. 1982. 'National Identity', in Carroll, John (ed.), *Intruders in the Bush: The Australian Quest for Identity*. Melbourne: Oxford University Press: 209-225.

Carter, Paul. 2010 [1987]. *Road to Botany Bay: An Exploration of Landscape and History*. Minneapolis: University of Minnesota Press.

Casey, Edward S. 1996. 'How to Get from Space to Place in a Fairly Short Stretch of Time: Phenomenological Prolegomena', in Feld, Steven and Keith H. Basso (eds), *Senses of Place*. Santa Fe: School of American Research Press: 13-52.

—. 1991. *Spirit and Soul: Essays in Philosophical Psychology*. Dallas: Spring Publications.

Cixous, Hélène. 2006. *Dream I Tell You* (tr. Beverley Bie Brahic). Edinburgh: Edinburgh University Press.

Clark, Nigel. 2003. 'Feral Ecologies: Performing Life on the Colonial Periphery', in Szerszynski, Bronislaw, Wallace Heim and Claire Waterton (eds), *Nature Performed: Environment, Culture and Performance*. Oxford and Malden: Blackwell Publishing: 163-182.

Clarke, Phillip A. 2007. *Aboriginal People and Their Plants*. Kenthurst: Rosenberg Publishing.

Code, Lorraine. 2006. *Ecological Thinking: The Politics of Epistemic Location*. Oxford and New York: Oxford University Press.

Cohen, Michael. 2006. 'Place and Dream-State: Spectacular Representations of Nationhood at Stadium Australia', in McAuley, Gay (ed.), *Unstable Ground: Performance and the Politics of Place*. Brussels: P.I.E. Peter Lang: 63-80.

Cowlishaw, Gillian. 2004. *Blackfellas Whitefellas and the Hidden Injuries of Race*. Oxford: Blackwell Publishing.

—. 1999. *Rednecks, Eggheads and Blackfellas: A Study of Racial Power and Intimacy in Australia*. Ann Arbor: The University of Michigan Press.

Cull, Laura. 2012. 'Performance as Philosophy: Responding to the Problem of "Application"'. *Theatre Research International* 37(1): 20-27.

Davidson, Robyn. 1998 [1980]. *Tracks*. Basingstoke and Oxford: Pan Macmillan Ltd.

Davis, Thulani. 2002. 'Theater Beyond Borders: Reconfiguring the Artist's Relationship to Community in the Twenty-First Century – Moving Beyond *Bantustans*', in Uno, Roberta and Lucy Mae San Pablo Burns (eds), *The Color of Theater: Race, Culture, and Contemporary Performance*. London and New York: Continuum: 21-26.

de Quincey, Tess. 2003. 'Burning Point: Overview Description of Triple Alice' in *About Performance* 5: 21-27.

—. 2011. Email Correspondence. 29 April.

—. 2005. Quoted in Fieldnotes. 25 July – 7 September.

Derrida, Jacques. 2006. *Geneses, Genealogies, Genres, and Genius: The Secrets of the Archive* (tr. Beverley Bie Brahic). Edinburgh: University of Edinburgh Press.

Dewey, John. 1910. *How We Think*. Boston et al: D.C. Heath & Co.

Dunn, Sarah. 2003. 'Triple Alice 1: A Participant's Perspective'. *About Performance* 5: 33-47.

Eco, Umberto. 1984. *The Role of the Reader: Explorations in the Semiotics of Texts*. Bloomington: Indiana University Press.

Edwards, Glenn, Benxiang Zeng, Keith Saalfeld, Petronella Vaarzon-Morel and Murray McGregor. 2008. *Managing the Impacts of Feral Camels in Australia: A New Way of Doing Business – Report 47*. Alice Springs: Desert Knowledge Cooperative Research Centre.

Entrikin, Nicholas J. 1991. *The Betweenness of Place: Towards a Geography of Modernity*. Baltimore: The John Hopkins University Press.

Etchells, Tim. 1999. *Certain Fragments: Contemporary Performance and Forced Entertainment*. London and New York: Routledge.

—. 2006. 'Blog: 27 May 2006'. On line at: http://www.forcedentertain ment.com/blog/ (consulted 01.06.2006).

Finnane, Kieran. 2005. 'Live Shows in Spades'. *Alice Springs News* (31 August 2005).

—. 1998. 'Performance "Lab" for Alice Artists' in *Alice Springs News* (26 August 1998).

Fleishman, Mark. 2012. 'The difference of performance as research' in *Theatre Research International* 37(1): 28-37.

Fraser, Peter. 1999. 'Triple Alice 1: Journal Entry 20 September 1999'. On line at: http://dequinceyco.net/TA/taframe01.htm (consulted 28.09.2013).

Freeman, Anthony. 2003. *Consciousness: A Guide to the Debates*. Santa Barbara, Denver and Oxford: ABC CLIO.

Gates, Laura Purcell. 2011. 'Locating the Self: Narratives and Pracitces of Authenticity in French Clown Training'. *Theatre, Dance and Performance Training* 2 (2): 231-242.

Gallasch, Keith with Tess de Quincey. 2000. 'Triple Alice: Catching the Weather'. *Real Time* 35: 9.

Goodall, Jane. 2006. 'Haunted Places', in McAuley, Gay (ed.) *Unstable Ground: Performance and the Politics of Place*. Brussels: P.I. E. Peter Lang: 111-124.

Grant, Stuart. 2002. 'Hot Talk in Central Australia'. *RealTime* 47: 9

Grant, Stuart, with Tess de Quincey. 2006. 'How to Stand in Australia', in McAuley, Gay (ed.), *Unstable Ground: Performance and the Politics of Place*. Brussels: P.I.E. Peter Lang.

Greer, Germaine. 2004. *Whitefella Jump Up: The Shortest Way to Nationhood*. London: Profile Books.

—. 2008. 'Once Upon a Time in a Land Far, Far Away'. *The Guardian* (15 December 2008).

Harrison, Kristina. 2003. 'From Observer to Participant: Reflections on the Triple Alice Experience'. *About Performance* 5: 13-20.

Harrison, Martin. 2000. 'Edge, Desert, Reticulation, Information'. *RealTime* 35: 8.

Haynes, Roslynn D. 1998. *Seeking the Centre: The Australian Desert in Literature, Art and Film*. Cambridge, New York and Melbourne: Cambridge University Press.

Hobson, J. Allan. 1988. *The Dreaming Brain: How the Brain Creates Both the Sense and the Nonsense of Dreams*. New York: Basic Books.

Hughes, Robert. 1987. *The Fatal Shore: A History of the Transportation of Convicts to Australia 1787-1868*. London: Pan Books.

Hunt, Victoria. 1999. 'Triple Alice 1: Journal Entry 9 October 1999'. On line at: http://dequinceyco.net/TA/taframe01.htm (consulted 28.09.2013).

Kaye, Nick. 2000. *Site-Specific Art: Performance, Place and Documentation*. London: Routledge.

Kwon, Miwon. 2002. *One Place After Another: Site-Specific Art and Locational Identity*. Cambridge and London: MIT Press.

Lacan, Jacques. 1997. *The Seminar of Jacques Lacan Book III: The Psychoses 1955-1956* (tr. Russell Grigg). New York and London: W.W. Norton & Co.

Lakoff, George and Mark Johnson. 1980. *Metaphors We Live By*. Chicago and London: The University of Chicago Press.

Lakoff, George and Mark Johnson. 1999. *Philosophy in the Flesh: The Embodied Mind and Its Challenge to Western Thought*. New York: Basic Books.

Langellier, Kristin. 1999. 'Personal Narrative, Performance, Performativity: Two of Three Things I know for Sure'. *Text and Performance Quarterly* 19: 125-144.

Levi-Strauss, Claude. 1966 [1962]. *The Savage Mind*. Chicago and London: The University of Chicago Press.

Lines, William J. 1991. *Taming the Great South Land: A History of the Conquest of Nature in Australia*. Athens and London: The University of Georgia Press.

Lippard, Lucy. 1997. *The Lure of the Local: Senses of Place in a Multicentered Society*. New York: New Press.

MacAloon, John J. 1984. 'Olympic Games and the Theory of Spectacle in Modern Societies', in MacAloon, John J. (ed.), *Rite, Drama, Festival, Spectacle: Rehearsals Toward a Theory of Cultural Performance*. Philadelphia: Institute for the Study of Human Issues: 241-280.

MacKenzie, Jeanne. 1961. *The Australian Paradox*. Melbourne: F.W. Cheshire.

Mackey, Sally. 2012. 'Of Lofts, Evidence and Mobile Times: The School Play as a Site of Memory'. *Research in Drama Education* 17 (1): 35-52.

Maher, Rachel. 2005. 'Deep in the Desert'. *RealTime* 69: 11.

Mahood, Kim. 2000. *Craft for a Dry Lake: A Memoir*. Sydney, Auckland, New York and London: Anchor Books.

Malpas, Jeff. 1999. *Place and Experience: A Philosophical Topography*. Cambridge: Cambridge University Press.

Martin, Jacqueline and Willmar Sauter. 2007. 'Playing Politics at the Adelaide Festival', in Hauptfleish, Temple et al. (eds). *Festivalising!: Theatrical Events, Politics and Culture*. Amsterdam: Rodopi: 97-118.

Massey, Doreen. 2005. *For Space*. London: Sage.

Maxwell, Ian. 2003. 'Access All Areas: Reflections on Triple Alice 1'. *About Performance* 5: 65-72

—. 2006. 'Parallel Evolution: Performance Studies at the University of Sydney'. *The Drama Review* 50(1): 33-45.

McAuley, Gay. 2003. 'Introduction' in *About Performance* 5: vii-xi.

—. 2000. 'Body Weather in the Central Desert of Australia: Towards an Ecology of Performance'. On line at: http://dequinceyco.net/wp-content/uploads/2010/10/gm-firt-2000.pdf (consulted 03.10.2013).

—. 2006. 'Introduction' in McAuley, Gay (ed.) *Unstable Ground: Performance and the Politics of Place*. Brussels: P.I.E. Peter Lang: 15-24.

McConachie, Bruce and F. Elizabeth Hart (eds). 2006. *Performance and Cognition: Theatre Studies and the Cognitive Turn*. Oxon and New York: Routledge.

McConcachie, Bruce. 2008. *Engaging Audiences: A Cognitive Approach te Spectating in the Theatre*. New York: Palgrave Macmillan.

Merleau-Ponty, Maurice. 2006 [1945]. *Phenomenology of Perception*. London and New York: Routledge.

Moon, Jennifer A. 2006 [1999]. *Learning Journals: A Handbook for Reflective Practice and Professional Development* (2nd Edition). New York: Routledge.

—. 1999. *Reflection in Learning and Professional Development*. London: Kogan Page.

Morton, Timothy. 2007. *Ecology Without Nature: Rethinking Environmental Aesthetics*. Cambridge and London: Harvard University Press.

Muecke, Stephen. 2002. 'The Fall: Fictocritical Writing'. *Parallax* 8(4): 108-112.

Neelands, Jonothan. 2004. 'Miracles Are Happening: Beyond the Rhetoric of Transformation in the Western Traditions of Drama Education'. *Research in Drama Education* 9 (1): 47-56.

Ness, Sally Ann. 1996. 'Dancing in the Field: Notes from Memory', in Foster, Susan Leigh (ed.), *Corporealities: Dancing Knowledge, Culture and Power*. London and New York: Routledge: 129-154.

Newman, Judith M. 2000. 'Action Research: A Brief Overview'. *Forum: Qualitative Social Research* 1 (1): np. On line at http://www.qualitative-research.net/index.php/fqs/article/view/1127/2507(consulted 20.07.2012).

Nora, Pierre. 1989. 'Between Memory and History: Les Lieux de Memoire' (tr. Marc Roudebush). *Representations* 26: 7-24.

Pelias, Ron. 1994. 'An Autobiographic Ethnography of Performance in Everyday Discourse'. *Journal of Dramatic Theory and Criticism* 8: 163-172.

Perera, Suvendrini and Joseph Pugliese. 2011. 'Death in a Dry River: Black Life, White Property, Parched Justice'. *Somatechnics* 1: 65-86.

Phelan, Peggy. 1995. 'Thirteen Ways of Looking at *Choreographing Writing*', in Foster, Susan Leigh (ed.), *Choreographing History*. Bloomington and Indianapolis: Indiana University Press: 200-210.

Pollock, Della. 1998. 'Performing Writing', in Phelan, Peggy and Jill Lane (eds), *The Ends of Performance*. New York: NYU Press: 73-103.

—. 1999. *Telling Bodies Performing Birth*. New York: Columbia University Press.

—. 2007. 'The Performative "I"'. *Cultural Studies <=> Critical Methodologies* 7: 239-255.

Prendergast, Monica. 2003. 'I, Me, Mine: Soliloquizing as Reflective Practice'. *International Journal of Education & the Arts* 4 (1): np. On line at: http://www.ijea.org/v4n1/index.html (consulted 26.06.2012).

Probyn, Elspeth. 2010. 'Writing Shame', in Gregg, Melissa and Gregory J. Seigworth (eds), *The Affect Theory Reader*. Durham: Duke University Press: 71-90.

Quon, Jane. 2004. 'Imaging Ocean Space: Marine Ecology and the Visual Arts in Tidal Interchange', in Lester, Libby and Claire Ellis (eds), *Conference Proceedings for Imaging Nature: Media, Environment and Tourism*. Hobart: University of Tasmania: np. On line at http://www.utas.edu.au/imaging/ (consulted 25.07.2007).

'RealTime-Performance Space Forum: Art Practice as Research' On line at: http://www.realtimearts.net/feature/RealTimePerformance_Space_Forums/8575 (consulted 25.09.2013).

Reynolds, Ann. 2004. 'Enantiomorphic Models', in Tsai, Eugenie Tsai with Cornelia Butler (eds), *Robert Smithson*. Berkeley, Los Angeles and London: University of California Press: 136-142.

Roach, Joseph. 1996. *Cities of the Dead: Circum-Atlantic Performance*. New York: Columbia University Press.

Rogers, Meredith. 2008. '*Musicircus* at the 2007 Melbourne International Arts Festival'. Paper presented at *Turangawaewae: A Sense of Place* (University of Otago: 30 June-3 July 2008).

Rose, Deborah Bird (ed.). 1995. *Country in Flames: Proceedings of the 1994 Symposium on Biodiversity and Fire in North Australia*. Canberra: Australian Government Department of Environment, Water, Heritage and the Arts.

Russo, Mary. 1994. *The Female Grotesque: Risk, Excess, and Modernity*. New York: Routledge.

Sack, Robert David. 1997. *Homo Geographicus: A Framework for Action, Awareness, and Moral Concern*. Baltimore and London: The Johns Hopkins University Press.

Saltz, David (ed.). 2007. *Performance and Cognition*. Special Issue of *Theatre Journal* 59 (4).

Schama, Simon. 1995. *Landscape and Memory*. New York: A.A. Knopf.

Schechner, Richard. *Between Theatre & Anthropology*. Philadelphia: University of Pennsylvania Press, 1985.

Schneider, Rebecca. 2011. *Performing Remains: Art and War in Times of Theatrical Reenactment*. London and New York: Routledge.

Schön, David. 1983. *The Reflective Practitioner*. New York: Basic Books.

—. 1987. *Educating the Reflective Practitioner*. San Francisco: Jossey-Bass.

Seddon, George. 1997. *Landprints: Reflections on Place and Landscape*. Cambridge, New York and Melbourne: Cambridge University Press.

Sellars, Peter. 2002. 'The Question of Culture', in Delgado, Maria M. and Caridad Svich (eds), *Theatre in Crisis? Performance Manifestos for a New Century*. Manchester and New York: Manchester University Press: 127-143.

Sellers-Young, Barbara. 1993. *Teaching Personality with Gracefulness: The Transmission of Japanese Cultural Values through Japanese Dance Theatre*. Lanham, New York and London: University Press of America.

—. 1998. 'Somatic Processes: Convergence of Theory and Practice'. *Theatre Topics* 8(2): 173-87.

Snow, Peter. 2002. *Imaging the In-Between: Training Becomes Performance in Body Weather Practice in Australia*. PhD Thesis. University of Sydney.

Spry, Tami. 2001. 'Performing Autoethnography: An Embodied Methodological Praxis'. *Qualitative Inquiry* 7 (6): 706-732.

Stanislavski, Konstantin. 1989[1936]. *An Actor Prepares* (tr. Elizabeth Reynolds Hapgood). New York: Routledge.

Stegner, Wallace. 2003. *Mormon Country* (2nd Edition). Lincoln: University of Nebraska Press.

Strehlow, T.G.H. 1961. *Nomads in No-Man's Land*. Adelaide: The Aborigines Advancement League, Inc.Stein, Bonnie Sue and Min Tanaka. 1986. 'Min Tanaka: Farmer/Dancer or Dancer/Farmer. An Interview'. *The Drama Review* 30 (2): 142-151.

Tanaka, Min. 1986. '*from* I Am an Avant-Garde Who Crawls the Earth: Homage to Tatsumi Hijikata'. *The Drama Review* 30 (2): 153-155.

Taylor, Diana. 2003. *The Archive and the Repertoire: Performing Cultural Memory in the Americas*. Durham and London: Duke University Press.

Taylor, Gretel. 2010. 'Empty? A Critique of the Notion of "Emptiness" in Butoh and Body Weather Training'. *Theatre, Dance and Performance Training* 1(1): 72-87.

Thompson, James. 2011. *Performance Affects: Applied Theatre and the End of Effect*. London: Palgrave Macmillan.

Tompkins, Joanne. 2007. *Unsettling Space: Contestations in Contemporary Australian Theatre*. New York: Palgrave Macmillan.

Trainor, Luke. 1994. *British Imperialism and Australian Nationalism: Manipulation, Conflict and Compromise in the Late Nineteenth Century*. New York: Cambridge University Press.

Tuan, Yi Fu. 1971. *Man and Nature*. Washington D.C.: Association of American Geographers.

Tuan, Yi Fu. 2001. 'The Desert and I: A Study in Affinity'. *Michigan Quarterly Review* 40: 7-16.

Turner, Victor. 1974. *Dramas, Fields, and Metaphors: Symbolic Action in Human Society*. Ithaca: Cornell University Press.

Vanclay, Frank. 2008. 'Place Matters', in Vanclay, Frank, Matthew Higgins and Adam Blackshaw (eds), *Making Sense of Place*. Canberra: National Museum of Australia: 3-11.

van de Ven, Frank. 2013. 'Body Weather Amsterdam'. On line at: http://bodyweather/amsterdam.blogspot.com (consulted 29.01.2013).

Vedel, Karen. 2007. 'Silica Tales and Other Moves in Lhere Mparntwe'. On line at: http://dequinceyco.net/media-archive/articles (consulted 5 October 2013).

Viala, Jean and Nourit Masson-Sekine. 1988. *Butoh: Shades of Darkness*. Tokyo: Shufunotomo Co., Ltd.

Woods, Peter. 1993. *Critical Events in Teaching and Learning*. London and Washington, D.C.: The Falmer Press.

Wyndham, Susan. 2007. 'Book Club: *Tracks* by Robyn Davidson'.*The Sydney Morning Herald* (21 January 2007). On line at: http://blogs.smh.com.au/entertainment/archives.undercover/009386.html (consulted 21.08.2013).

Zeki, Semir. 1999. *Inner Vision: An Exploration of Art and the Brain*. Oxford: Oxford University Press.

Index